Performance, Art, and Politics in the African Diaspora

This book examines necropolitics and performance art, with a particular focus on the black body and the African diaspora.

In this book, Myron M. Beasley situates artists as cultural workers and theorists who illuminate the political linkages between their own and others' specific locales. The focus is an interrogation of the political systems that dictate and determine the value of lives (and decide which lives matter) through a lens of performance and art. Beasley highlights how the performances of rupture, which are of artistic and historical significance, reveal both strategies of survival and promises of possibility. Artists and curators examined include Jelili Atiku, Giscard Bouchotte, Nona Faustine, Vanessa German, Simone Leigh, Nathalie Anguezomo Mba Bikoro, Ebony G. Patterson, and Dianne Smith.

The volume is an ideal research and reference book for students and scholars of Contemporary Art, African Studies, and Performance Theory.

Myron M. Beasley is Associate Professor of American Studies and Gender and Sexuality Studies at Bates College.

Routledge Focus on Art History and Visual Studies

Routledge Focus on Art History and Visual Studies presents short-form books on varied topics within the fields of art history and visual studies.

World-Forming and Contemporary Art
Jessica Holtaway

The Power and Fluidity of Girlhood in Henry Darger's Art
Leisa Rundquist

Buckminster Fuller's World Game and Its Legacy
Timothy Stott

Post-Digital Letterpress Printing
Research, Education and Practice
Edited by Pedro Manuel Reis Amado, Ana Catarina Silva and Vítor Quelhas

Bodily Engagements with Film, Images, and Technology
Somavision
Max Ryynänen

Performance, Art, and Politics in the African Diaspora
Necropolitics and the Black Body
Myron M. Beasley

For more information about this series, please visit: https://www.routledge.com/Routledge-Focus-on-Art-History-and-Visual-Studies/book-series/FOCUSAH

Performance, Art, and Politics in the African Diaspora

Necropolitics and the Black Body

Myron M. Beasley

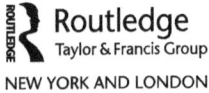
Routledge
Taylor & Francis Group

NEW YORK AND LONDON

First published 2023
by Routledge
605 Third Avenue, New York, NY 10158

and by Routledge
4 Park Square, Milton Park, Abingdon, Oxon, OX14 4RN

Routledge is an imprint of the Taylor & Francis Group, an informa business

© 2023 Taylor & Francis

The right of **Myron M. Beasley** to be identified as the author of this Work has been asserted in accordance with sections 77 and 78 of the Copyright, Designs and Patents Act 1988.

Trademark notice: Product or corporate names may be trademarks or registered trademarks, and are used only for identification and explanation without intent to infringe.

Library of Congress Cataloging-in-Publication Data
Names: Beasley, Myron, author.
Title: Performance, art and politics in the African diaspora : necropolitics and the Black body / Myron Beasley.
Description: New York, NY : Routledge, 2023. | Includes bibliographical references and index.
Identifiers: LCCN 2022059858 (print) | LCCN 2022059859 (ebook) | ISBN 9780367136925 (hardback) | ISBN 9781032417707 (paperback) | ISBN 9780429028489 (ebook)
Subjects: LCSH: Performance art. | Death in art. | Art and society. | African diaspora.
Classification: LCC NX456.5.P38 B43 2023 (print) | LCC NX456.5.P38 (ebook) | DDC 709.040755—dc23/eng/20221213
LC record available at https://lccn.loc.gov/2022059858
LC ebook record available at https://lccn.loc.gov/2022059859

ISBN: 9780367136925 (hbk)
ISBN: 9781032417707 (pbk)
ISBN: 9780429028489 (ebk)

DOI: 10.4324/9780429028489

Typeset in Times New Roman
by codeMantra

To Martha. I am here because of you.

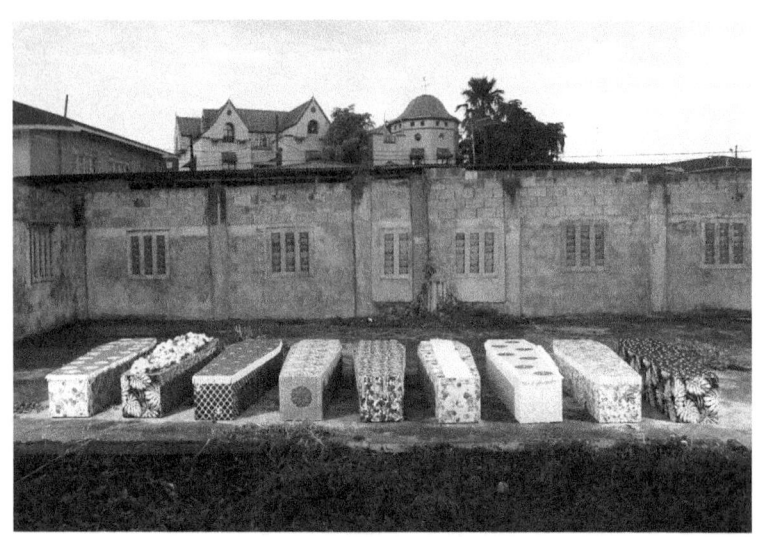

Contents

Acknowledgments

I am thankful for the "village" of people and organizations who have provided such support, encouragement, and love to make this project happen. I am honored by awards and grants from the following organizations that provided the support to do this work: The Andy Warhol Foundation Arts Writers Grant, Ruth Landes Memorial Research Fund (Reed Foundation), Whiting Foundation, Dorothea and Leo Rabkin Foundation, and Bates Faculty Development Fund. This project was birthed while serving as the first scholar in residence at SAVVY Contemporary in Berlin and further developed and completed at Hewnoaks and Monson Arts residencies. Thank you for providing the time and space to contemplate and develop this research.

I am grateful for being awarded two visiting professorships where students and faculty provided support and in-depth conversations about several topics addressed in this manuscript. My friends at the University of Montevallo in Alabama—where I occupied the Paschal P. Vacca Chair of the Liberal Arts, thank you, especially to Tonja Battle, for your support and encouragement. And the graduate program in American Studies at the University of Bamberg in Germany, Chair Christine Gerhardt, you've been a great source of enthusiasm and support since graduate school.

I am grateful for intellectual and creative partners who have engaged me with conversations and advice about this work: Lewis Gordon, Rebecca Herzig, Erica Rand, Melinda Plastas, Anne Hallward, James Rough, Kristen Barnett, Antonio Lucio Rodrigues de Jesus, Susan Larson, Susan Farnsworth, Lesly Percil, Jean-Elie Gilles, Jordan Corey, Marcus Bruce, Arlette Frund, Bonnie Porta, Danielle Conway, Bonaventure Soh Bejeng Ndikung, Joshua Shain, Quinlan Miller, Michel Droge and my American Studies, and Gender and Sexuality Studies colleagues at Bates College. Camille Hazeur and Diana Hayman thank you for your love and support not to mention providing housing to write in New Orleans and Quebec City. Valerie Kabov and Marcus Gora and the crew at the First Floor Gallery in Harare, Zimbabwe, hosted the first AFiRIperFOMA Biennial, where I witnessed the most beautifully nuanced performance art by artists from the continent of Africa. And where I met Lotte Løevholm, who introduced me to Jelili, thank you. I love librarians! The project would have been impossible without the help of Laura Juraska, Chris Schiff, and Christina Bell. And to the always generous, thoughtful, and encouraging crew in the print and post office at Bates College, Edward Jawor and Laurie Anderson, thank you.

I appreciate and am so thankful for the hands who have fed me and provided endless cups of coffee: The staff of Slates and Coffee by Design, who know me as the guy who sits and writes, and Kirk Henry and Troy Lopez of RosaColeta in Berlin and my lovely Roseline Senatus of the Hotel Florita in Jacmel, Haiti—who always takes good care of me.

I am grateful for the generosity of the artists who are featured in this project: Jelili Atiku, Giscard Bouchotte, Dianne Smith, Nona Faustine, Vanessa German, Simone Leigh, and Ebony G. Patterson— who gave their time for interviews and, in some instances, allowed me to follow them for days. You are cultural workers who continue to inspire me and others. To Isabelle Viti and Katie Armstrong of Routledge/Taylor and Francis, UK, thank you for believing in this project and for your patience. To Ilana Rosker, who was able to perform her organizational wizardry in the final stages of this project.

Thank you, Jane Anna Gordon, who provided such generous and insightful editorial and intellectual feedback that helped shape this project. To my BFFs, Yoon Soo Lee and Jean-Paul Rocchi, who taught me the true meaning of friendship and how to practice love. Thank you to my family for their continued support. To Pat Hager, my thought partner in Maine, who is always generous with her rhetorical, writing, and intellectual opinions, to whom I am most indebted.

Foreword

What does art offer to communities beset by unrelenting trage-
dies? Nothing less than a resounding affirmation of a distinctively
human creative resilience; an echoing insistence to live and to live
with a dignity that is regal.

With his characteristic attention to when the beautiful and the
powerful meet, in the text that follows, Myron M. Beasley invites
you to journey with him.

From processionals of the Sisterhood of Our Lady of Good Death
in annual celebration in the cobbled streets of Cachoeira, Brazil ...
to refurbished cargo boxes in Jacmel that challenge Haiti as "open
for business" with it instead welcoming dreaming ... to the parade
of caskets through Port of Spain, Trinidad, accompanied by Pita
Pata and eulogies of the recently deceased... to artist Nona Faustine, wearing only white shoes, as she stands on a wooden block
erected at the central intersection on Wall Street where enslaved
Africans were sold ... to a bare, living body buried beneath stones
on a mountain in Chihuahua, Mexico, where victims of femicide
frequently remain ... to a Victorian house painted sky-blue in Pittsburgh and rehabbed as an open space for intergenerational creativity for BIPOC children, adults, and artists ...

Centering art as *doing*, as *generating agitation* in pursuit of a
greater good, Beasley celebrates when creative performances actively
erode conventions that would sever the physical and the spiritual, the
secular and the sacred, the functional and the aesthetic, the African
Diaspora and the African, the present and the past, and the still living
and the no longer. Replete with rich portraits of artists who activate
our environments, pressing us to ponder the relationship between
concealment and revelation, revilement and celebration, collective
forgetting, and candid remembering, not hearing and really listening,
graveyards and gardens, Beasley shows how communal creative productions enable us to feel the persistent lingering of what has come
before so that we can make known to ourselves and to others the

unmarked, unseen, and unsaid. Such dynamic truth-telling enables us to face our ghosts and to ingest what howls and haunts so that our response to the brutalities that birthed our worlds is not continued amnesia.

Stitched through is a meditation on the meaning of a fitting burial, of how to usher bodies emptied of spirit honorably to what is next; of how communities marked by a ubiquity of untimely, brutal loss assure that such transitions are holy. After all, if uncared for, even in death the horrors of life will persist.

Beasley knows that *becoming* is no easy process. In Black and Indigenous contexts where violent death is more regularized than dialogue and human bodies are reduced to corpses as they are left on hills and streets and floors by deliberate withholding of care, rituals, at their best, reach to the realm of ancestral guides with art serving as an intermediary. Preparing the eye with what sparkles and allures, the work that is Beasley's focus creates radically hospitable places for people made home—and land-less, who still, in their accent, gait, and voice enact a stubborn "yes, still."

In a work of scholarship that helps us to hear what is near and still unfamiliar, Beasley offers succor we sorely need: Performances of possibility; refusals to surrender to narratives or fates of debasement, a yearning expressed in deeds for what can and will be. Such are the theaters through which we actively bury monuments to the murderous mayhem that erected Euro modernity and its long shadows that we still inhabit. Such are the theaters that cultivate the sacredness of daily existence where art is lived in and as rest, resistance, and renewal.

—Jane Anna Gordon

1 Performance, Death, Politics

Marked by the processional of the Irmandade Nossa Senhora da Boa Morte (or Sisterhood of Our Lady of the Good Death), Festa da Boa Morte is an annual celebration held in the small historic town of Cachoeira, Brazil, to commemorate "a good death" (Katz). The Sisterhood, which is a collective of seventy-five plus year-old women, was established in 1820 by Jesuit priests as one of many confraternities whose purpose was to convert and assimilate enslaved Africans. While some did their bidding, other confraternities became places of resistance, where performances of traditional African-based faiths were retained and practiced through rituals that were officially Catholic. With a history spanning back to the period of enslavement, the members of this collective are dedicated to honoring and responding to the treatment of enslaved bodies that were tossed as detritus into the mass grave of the sea. "The good death," for the Sisterhood, is one marked by "a fitting burial place and funeral, as to usher the body into the spiritual realm with honor" (Katz). Their annual walk through the cobbled stone village is a performative action that recalls the denial of such a dignified return to the bodies of black people brought forcefully to the Americas. If "the good death" is about a specifically human transition from this—worldly life, securing it is to be freed from the past and present horrors of enslavement.

In 2009, Artist Dread Scott walked the streets of New York City holding a placard that read: "I am not a man" (Scott). Evoking the imagery of the African American sanitation workers strike in Memphis of 1968, where the men repeatedly shouted, "I am a man" to demand equal standing in the economic and social spheres of the United States of their day, Scotts' insertion, fifty years later, of the word "not," suggests the continued black struggle for fitting recognition as human beings.

DOI: 10.4324/9780429028489-1

The walks of the Sisterhood and of Scott are separated by geography but linked by a shared lineage of New World people of African descent who publicly pose questions about what it means for them to try to live and to die with dignity in an anti-black world. Both sets of performative action respond to the cultural, economic, and political faces of structural systems that refuse to acknowledge the existence of black lives as human lives. The Sisterhood does this through their mission of providing a proper burial for black bodies. An annual memorial of the significance of their task forces the many tourists who invade their small town to see death as a living topic inseparable from the economics and the political systems that endorsed and sustained the commercial endeavor of slavery and its many contemporary legacies. So when Cathy Cohen proclaims, "death is not a new phenomenon in black communities," she refers to the specific history of struggle and anti-black politics that exist in the world (xi).

This book contributes to the vibrant field of black existentialism through exploring artistic interrogations of death produced by members of the African Diaspora. I contend and will illustrate that this work destabilizes conventional Western-dominated ideas about the relationship among death, value, humanity, art, and performance. As Kobena Mercer has long argued, I frame artists as cultural workers who illuminate the political linkages between their own and other specific locales throughout the black diaspora (2016). Specifically, in the following pages, I highlight how their performances of rupture, which are of art historical significance, reveal both strategies of survival and promises of possibility.

Consider the Jerome Project by Titus Kaphar (2014). In 2011, Kaphar set out to look for his incarcerated father. Searching online for his father's prison record, he learned of the plethora of readily accessible websites featuring both the records and the images of the incarcerated. Among them Kaphar discovered dozens of individuals who shared both his father's first name, Jerome, as well as his last name (Keith). Inspired by the magnitude of these criminal visual representation of black men, Kaphar created panels with portraits of the men before gold leaf backgrounds that parallel Byzantine sacred images. Each portrait is then dipped in different depths of tar, corresponding with the length of time the individual was imprisoned. The tar extends up to the men's mouths to offer cover and to represent previously denied privacy from the public sharing of their mug shots. Simultaneously, the tar symbolizes their lingering silence that takes the form of the stripping of voting rights, jobs, and access to state and federally funded programs. As a statement about the criminal industrial complex, the project juxtaposes "the use of policing and imprisonment by the US government as a means to address economic, social and political problems," with St. Jerome, the patron saint of libraries and scholars, also known as the confessor, who believed in absolution and the power of redemption (Keith). Kaphar's ritual of painting individual portraits and dipping the images in the tar was an act of acknowledging the personhood of each man and a condemnation of the US criminal justice system for its lack of forgiveness and repatriation. Kaphar puts his personal quest to find his father into dialog with broader historic and contemporary questions of religion and social justice. Like the Sisterhood and Scott, he asks both what a fitting human response would be to economic, social, and political problems and what we do in the face of its denial.

These works and others explored in further detail in the chapters that follow probe the central questions raised by attendees, including myself, of the 2014 AFiRIperFOMA Biennial in Harare, Zimbabwe. Billed as the first performance art conference of its kind on the continent of Africa and curated and directed by international Nigerian artist Jelili Atiku, it brought together some of the most poetic and aesthetically nuanced performance art I have ever witnessed, all by artists from various African countries (Atiku). Many attendees, particularly those of us who reside in the West, were confronted anew with questions about the nature of both performance and of art when pursued with the epistemological and ontological tenets of various Africana cosmologies in which the line between the sacred and secular is thin and the space between function and aesthetic is often indecipherable (Gordon 2002, Somé 1997). As Cameroonian artist Trésor Malaya's plastic and yarned wrapped body glided across the roof of the high-rise buildings, creating a trail of dots from the red paint trickling from his body, the audience was asked to follow the freshly smeared marks. As Malaya arrived at a wall where he scrawled, "No, No," using his paint covered hand, the audience was handed eggs and encouraged to throw them against the freshly scribbled words. Titled 21 and reflecting the number of deaths by the Cameroon military police during a recent protest for water rights, the piece was the most evocative performance at the conference and triggered the political attention of the local military authorities. When I asked Malaya about his training as a performance artist, he quipped, "Performance what? This is nothing more than ritual." Disrupting prevailing epistemological and aesthetic distinctions of what is defined as art and what is ritual, Malaya's work also complicates the current preoccupation in the United States and Europe with community engaged art, relational art, or even socially engaged practice.

Claiming his performance was ritual signaling Malaya's collapsing of the personal and the political. Not only using his body as an instrument in the performance, but he also portrays it as the site of suffering in the face of the issue of water rights to which his ritual responds, where suffering involves the ability to recognize the "political realities of one's condition" (Gordon). Ritual, according to Somé, is an action that acknowledges and thereby makes present one's ancestral lineage for the sake of personal healing and the healing of "the suffering of the world" (1997). Put differently, it seeks connection with external forces outside of the human realm (including gods and ancestors) that will simultaneously, according to Gordon, maintain and nurture community. The discussion in the following pages foregrounds the work of artists who are interpreting experiences where the local and global rub up against one another so that their work suggests strategies for survival and resistance that are locally meaningful and that can travel. They also blur or eradicate the distinction between the secular and the sacred, framing artistic production as intertwined with the fabric of everyday life which is seamlessly suffused with the elements from the domains of religion, cultural traditions, and politics.

Take, for instance, David Hammons (Hassan, 2008) "art piece" submission to the Dakar Biennale in which he orchestrated a two-week sheep raffle in the middle of the busiest intersections of Dakar. Fashioning the raffle tickets in the form of Senegalese banknotes, he announced the raffle, "Tombola de Moutons," in Woloff, French, and English on billboards throughout Dakar. The performance was multilayered. A protest against international art fairs sold as an economic engine in developing communities asphyxiated by economic global policies inaugurated by Euro-modern colonization, Hammons explained, "people in Dakar do not go to exhibitions. They think that the Dak'Art is for white people. At least, with the Sheep Raffle, I'll give them something that they can relate to" (2008). And the artist did give away two sheep a day in a place where such a resource really mattered. The performance also critiqued capitalism run amok in the West as only weeks earlier Oprah commenced her nineteenth season by giving away cars to her studio audience. Giving away sheep, and specifically the white sheep revered in Yoruba, Dogon, and Muslim traditional religious practices, also signaled a ritual with sacred significance. In sacrificial language that was locally meaningful, Hammons spoke across the African Diaspora through art about the material terms of survival.

In both Zimbabwe and Senegal, as in Cachoeira and New York City, the artists I write about draw from a variety of genres. When I call their work "performance," I do so to describe the work, actions, and the creative processes of the artists. In other words, the concept of "performance" in this text is not limited to the art object, project, or output, but foregrounds the *doing* and the engagement *with*. The specific corpus of material garnered in this book are derived from my own ethnographic fieldwork in various locations in the African Diaspora. All center oppositional discourses and forms of resistance against lingering colonial moral codes and restrictive global economic laws within supposedly post-colonial regimes. In each instance, while working in certain locales, I witnessed and began working with artists who were attending to these issues through creative actions. For instance, as explored in Chapter 2, while doing fieldwork in Jacmel, Haiti on the topic of underground food economic systems and how a collective of street food vendors usurped imposed regulatory laws to feed the hungry, I became engrossed with the work of curator Giscard Bouchotte, who organized artists to stage creative actions throughout the small town. The work of Ruth Landes and Zora Neale Hurston paved the way for me to engage with the cultural politics of African aesthetics and performance as worthy points of investigation that reveal the structural politics of a particular community. Landes' methodology as well as the subjects of her ethnographic work with the women of the Ojibwa community and 1947 study of same-sex desire and ritual performance in the African-based faith, Candomblé, profoundly influenced my academic career. Similarly, Zora Neale Hurston, the consummate performance ethnographer, who in the moment when she performs her ethnographic interviews before Boas, shifted the domain of ethnographic inquiry, placing the "I" and corporality of the researcher in the ethnographic project. Both scholars embraced a transdisciplinary approach to humanistic inquiry, or one in which, according to Gordon, "disciplines work through each other ... to go beyond disciplines in the production of knowledge" (2012). Both Landes and Hurston faced discipline and temporary exile from the academy for questioning prevailing methods and not privileging disciplinary boundaries. In their productions of knowledge, they constructed platforms through which would-be subjects emerged as co-researchers able to speak for themselves, thereby offering examples of creative and novel ways of presenting academic scholarship. Finally, in so doing, Landes and Hurston humanized people of African descent and Indigenous communities. In this endeavor, I work through the areas of art history and criticism, cultural studies, Africana thought and performance theory as to propose the generative nature of the artists' work. As I write about the artists and their work, the writing will reflect my dwelling in such places and working alongside the artists and their communities and witnessing the cultural politics surrounding the performative actions. Thus, I document and engage the creatively imaginative range of possibility permitted from the ruptures caused by the artists.

In the essay titled "Creative Process" published in 1962 at the behest of then President John Kennedy, iconic African American writer and public intellectual James Baldwin charged his contemporary artists with assuming the position of "disturbers of the peace" (Baldwin). At a time of political and social unrest during the civil rights movement, Baldwin insisted that artists, as the conscience of society, were responsible for "correct[ing] the delusions" that we live in a stable world (6). To do so, the artist had to recall and "let us know, that there is nothing stable under heaven." Although Baldwin's audience was artists who resided in the United States, his statement remains salient to artists globally. After all, there are still systems and structures of oppression to which artists must turn our attention.

For Baldwin, artists as cultural workers were particularly entrusted with the responsibility of agitation, not for the sake of agitation but to contribute to the unraveling of societal injustices. The interpretation of artists as cultural workers can be broadly construed, but, for this endeavor, my interest rests with artists consumed with (but not limited only to) political interventions, community engagement, and matters of accessibility—artists that disdain "art for art's sake" and pursue art for the sake of nurturing political consciousness and movement toward social change (Jackson).[1] In this sense, I give pride of place to artists who, according to Nato Thompson's definition, "work more comfortably on the street and within a community of activists than in the gallery" (Nato Thompson). At the same time, as I will illuminate, embracing the blurring of the aesthetic and the functional, the sacred and the secular means that we must treat what will count as "political" or "community engaged" as open. What we can say in advance is that our "disturbers of the peace" are all engaged with interrogating the persistent precarity of people of African descent around the world and devising ways to value life in the face of these profound challenges.

Artists as Cultural Workers

In 2014 at the Copenhagen International Film Festival, Joshua Oppenheimer stated that "journalism is there to tell us what we need to know. Art is there to show us what we already know, but don't discuss." The artists discussed in this book, are citizens who endeavor discomfort to promote cultural and political awareness to encourage dialog. They are cultural workers because they are astutely aware of the awesome responsibility to produce and create work that represent the good and the evil of humanity. The artists featured in the chapters that follow are from sites in the African Diaspora as diverse as their mediums and the range of political and social issues addressed in their artistic productions. Each chapter foregrounds a different artist.

The focus of Chapter 2 is curator, Giscard Bouchotte, and his project "Haiti is for Dreaming," an exhibition curated in Jacmel, Haiti (dos Santos; Paravisini). The installation is a series of cargo shipping containers in each of which an artist critically responds to the declaration, "Haiti is open for Business," espoused by Bill and Hillary Clinton and then Haitian President Martelly at a televised ribbon-cutting presentation that occurred a few months after the devastating earthquake. They announced a different kind of ground-breaking,—a tax-free zone industrial park, even as the country continued to suffer from the ill effects of Non-governmental organizations (NGOs) on the island. Endorsed by the Clinton Foundation, the industrial park was to be built on what is considered the most fertile farmland and the area of a distinguished farming tradition in Haiti. Farmers and their families were forcibly moved and given stipends, while their land was transferred to international corporations who promised economic growth by creating sweatshops. "Haiti is for Dreaming" critiques the invasion of NGOs and imposed stringent economic policies of international banking in post-earthquake Haiti and the warped models for economic growth that center sweatshops and tax-free zones. Bouchotte summons artists to present alternatives in their cargo boxes. Through so doing, they disturb the peace surrounding repressive economic systems, and contributors also provide different ways of imagining, daring Haitians to dream of possibilities and futures.

In Chapter 3, I discuss municipal interference in the funeral performance by Jamaican artist, Ebony G. Patterson (2011). Known for her "blinging" tapestries of multilayered portraitures of cloth, beads, and glitter that play with Jamaican dance hall culture, Patterson's work skews the gender and sexuality of her subjects to entice with the aesthetic yet blatantly challenge the onlooker. When she arrived in Port of Spain, Trinidad, at the Alice Yard Art Center in June 2011, she was confronted with the all-too-familiar realities of the recurring senseless deaths of black men. In this chapter, I discuss the "9 of 219," a funeral performance through the streets of Trinidad where Patterson sought to bring disruptive attention to the deaths of black men through orchestrating a parade of blinged coffins around the island with walkers chanting traditional Trinidadian mourning songs. Her work became a site of resistance as members of the municipal government physically attempted to prevent the performance.

Harlem-based artist Dianne Smith is the focus of Chapter 4. I consider Smith's use of paper and archival visual images to address the politics of gentrification and the death of black culture in Harlem. The chapter outlines the political systems set in place to allow for the current wave of "redevelopment" responsible for the rapidly deceasing black populations. Further, I situate three installations ("Between Harlem and Me", "Uptown Parade," and "STUFF") by Smith as strategies to preserve the black history of Harlem and her response to gentrification.

In Chapter 5, I focus on Nona Faustine's "White Shoe" photo series, which challenges the effort of New York City to erase the history of its slave sites (Faustine et al.). Playing with the archive, Faustine channels Saärtjie "Sarah" Baartman, known as Venus Hottentot, projecting her nude body on specific, highly public, and visible sites in the city, such as Wall Street, the City Hall, and the Supreme Court. Faustine's performance complicates the meaning and politics of the archive by exploring when it is made absent and how it is represented visually. By imposing the photographic image of Baartman's body in central of landmarks of New York City, Faustine disrupts existing norms about what gets remembered and why.

Chapter 6 focuses on artist Nathalie Anguezomo Mba Bikoro. Born and reared in Gabon, educated in France and England, and currently residing in Berlin, her "After Sundance" a durational performance at the Venice Biennale, addresses colonial memory and denounces the post-colonial treatment of indigenous communities of North America. Derived from a ritual of several native communities in the United States and Canada, "After Sundance" is a requiem and a warning against the continued disregard of the cultures and histories of native communities.

In Chapter 7, I turn to Nigerian-based artist Jelili Atiku's preoccupation with human rights and his performance, *Aragamago, We Rid This Land Off Terrorism*. The durational community-based performance is a response to the treatment of women in his community in Nigeria. Atiku's work is unapologetically situated in the Yoruba faith. As his faith undergirds his practice, it complicates the meaning of performance art and welcomes a discussion about decolonization. His inclination to "performance art is my quest for self-decolonization." Atiku's art foregrounds an indigenous knowledge system that works to decenter a Western-dominated reading of art and art history.

Finally, I conclude with a discussion on healing the body with Vanessa German and Simone Leigh. In 2010, German invested her own money to purchase and renovate a house in Pittsburgh, Pennsylvania, to allow young people in the neighborhood to engage in art as a way of healing and dealing with trauma. "The Waiting Room" was a 2016 exhibition at the New Museum, where Simone Leigh places central focus on black women and the failure of health care system to care for their bodies. As an intervention, the piece recalls the violent and painful histories of treatment of black bodies by medical practitioners while also providing solutions. As such, the museum becomes a place for healing, challenging both the meaning and potential uses of the medical industry and the institution of the museum.

When the police officer in the Eric Garner case was not indicted, art critic David Joselit responded by saying both that it was a reminder of the continued racial inequality of the US legal systems and that, given the highly circulated videos of what transpired with Garner and of other instances of violence against black bodies, the verdict was also an indictment against conceptual art (Joselit). I would suggest that it is instead an indictment of a monolithic reading and a limited definition of conceptual art that has long supported anti-black discourses and ignored the kinds of work and themes explored in this book. For these performance artists, the success or failure of their work does not hinge on the ability to keep people alive or secure just outcomes, though this is certainly a hope. It is instead about how to cope with a norm of the denial of justice while nurturing a capacity to continue through exploring the interplay of death and freedom in the face of persistent black precarity.

Note

1 While Jackson's comprehensive historiography of the economic and governmental policies that gave rise to the language of social and welfare concerns and how artists have both critiqued "social reforms" and in many ways supported and benefited from the discourse of austerity, it is the labor and scholarship of Nato Thompson (2017, 2015, 2006), who has written exhaustively on the topic of art and activism, particularly situating art engagement in Marxist and critical theories that informs this work. The New Museum's "Social Works" (2017) does more to align the political theory with art and activism. The Vera List Center for Art and Politics at the New School, since 1992 has stated as its purpose "explore the role of the arts in developing a civic culture of tolerance and pluralism in the United States." This project will allow for a discussion of how such work is configured in locations of the African Diaspora, where concepts of "social work," "welfare," and government assistance do not exist.

Works Cited

Atiku, Jelili. *1st Afiriperfoma Biennial* https://biennialfoundation.org/2013/09/1st-afiriperfoma-biennial-will-mainly-focus-on-the-african-continent-the-culture-and-its-people-as-observed-by-artists-through-a-contemporary-visual-outlook/.

Baldwin, James. *The Price of the Ticket: Collected Nonfiction, 1948–1985.* St. Martin's Press, 1985.

Bikoro Mba Anguezomo, Nathalie. *After Sundance; on Indigenous Resistance* http://www.anguezomo-bikoro.com/after-sundance-on-indigenous-resistance.html. Accessed March 24 2022.

Cohen, Cathy J. *The Boundaries of Blackness: Aids and the Breakdown of Black Politics.* University of Chicago Press, 1999.

dos Santos, Matilde. "(In)Visibilité Ostentatoire, Conversation Avec Le Commissaire Giscard Bouchotte." *Aica Caraïbe du Sud* https://aica-sc.net/2017/07/28/invisibilite-ostentatoire-conversation-avec-le-commissaire-giscard-bouchotte/. Accessed March 24 2022.

Edwards, Brent Hayes. *The Practice of Diaspora: Literature, Translation, and the Rise of Black Internationalism.* Harvard University Press, 2003.

Faustine, N. et al. *White Shoes.* Mackaware, 2021.

Gordon, Leah. "The Sculptors of Grand Rue." *Raw Vision*, vol. 65, 2008, pp. 44–47.

Gordon, Lewis. "Obligations across Generations: A Consideration in the Understanding of Community Formation." *Diversity and Community: An Interdisciplinary Reader.* Ed. Philip Alperson. Malden, MA: Blackwell Pub., 2002. xiii, p. 351

Hammons, David Hammons David Campos-Pons Maria Magdalena Z. Pamela Hassan Salah M. Finley Cheryl Dak'art. *Diaspora Memory Place: David Hammons, Maria Magdalena Campos-Pons, Pamela Z.* Prestel: Prince Claus Fund Library, 2008.

Jackson, S. *Social Works: Performing Art, Supporting Publics*. Routledge, 2011.

Joselit, David. "Material Witness: David Joselit on Visual Evidence and the Case of Eric Garner." *Artforum International Magazine*, vol. 53, no. 6, 2015, p. 202.

Kaphar, Titus. "The Jerome Project (My Loss)." *Brooklyn Museum* https://www.brooklynmuseum.org/opencollection/objects/218233. Accessed March 24 2022.

Katz, Naomi. "Irmande De Boa Morte-Brazil's Sisterhood of Our Lady of Good Death." *The World and I (November)*, 1990, pp. 663–73.

Keith, Naima J. "Wall Text." *The Jerome Project*. Studio Museum of Harlem https://tinyurl.com/2ujw545b. Accessed February 9, 2022.

Landes, Ruth. *The Ojibwa Woman*. Columbia University Press, 1938.

Mercer, Kobena. *Travel & See: Black Diaspora Art Practices Since the 1980s*. Duke University Press, 2016. vol. Book, Whole.

Oppenheimer, Joshua. *Copenhagen International Film Festival*. November 6–16, 2014. https://arterritory.com/en/screen_-stage/topical_qa/12166-copenhagen_international_documentary_film_festival_cphdox/. Accessed February 12 2022.

Paravisini, Lisa. "Art Exhibit: Haiti Kingdom of This World." *Repeating Islands* https://repeatingislands.com/2011/11/20/art-exhibit-haiti-kingdom-of-this-world/. Accessed March 24 2022.

Patterson, Ebony G. "The Coffins That Moved." *9 out of 219 Alice Yard Art Center* https://pleasurett.blogspot.com/2011/07/coffins-that-moved.html. Accessed March 24 2022.

Scott, Dread. "I Am Not a Man." *Dread Scott* https://www.dreadscott.net/portfolio_page/i-am-not-a-man/. Accessed February 9 2022.

Somé, Malidoma Patrice. *Ritual: Power, Healing and Community*. Penguin, 1997.

Thompson, Nato. *Culture as Weapon: The Art of Influence in Everyday Life*. Melville House, 2017.

2 Haiti Is Open for Dreaming/Haiti Is Open for Business

Curating Périféeriques against Precarity

Because art must not be outside the primary concerns of people and it opens up a space that appeals to our collective imagination, the artists and organizations that produce them have an important role in the production of meaning. And this time we chose the city of Jacmel. Périféeriques # 3 is part of the dynamic of a better consideration of the public space in Haiti. Entirely free, Périféeriques is an opportunity to discover new aesthetics, new discourses, new ways of doing things in a context where the collective interest is rarely considered.[1]

—"Périféeriques: We are open for Dreaming"

On October 22, 2012, almost two years after the devastating earthquake shattered the island, Michel Martelly, the newly elected president of Haiti stood with Bill and Hillary Clinton at his side, proudly opening the 600-acre Caracol Industrial Park; "What is happening here in Caracol is already having ripple effects that will create jobs and opportunities far beyond this industrial park," proclaimed the US Secretary of State, Hillary Clinton to the perfectly arranged crowd that included celebrities such as Sean Penn and Danna Karan. The former US President Bill Clinton stood beaming as the proposed project was to become the symbol of the recovery efforts for Haiti. After years of negotiations, the project was a collaboration between the US State Department, the Inter-American Development Bank, the William J. Clinton Foundation, and Sae-A Trading, a Korean-based clothing company. Martelly would conclude the event by announcing, "Haiti is open for Business!" Watching the televised production, Haitian born curator Giscard Bouchotte, who only months earlier had returned to Haiti after curating the first pavilion representing the Republic of Haiti at the Venice Biennale, observing in disappointment, yelled after Martelly's remarks, "No, Haiti is for dreaming!"

DOI: 10.4324/9780429028489-2

I arrived in Haiti in 2002 to conduct fieldwork in the city of Jacmel. My engagement with the community led to curating and writing about Haitian artists and social policy. In December 2009, I was part of a curatorial team for an art fair that took place in the Grand Rue neighborhood of Port-Au-Prince. The event concluded and I departed just several days before the earthquake of January 12, 2010. I witnessed the already NGO flooded country become a tsunami of international aid organizations eager to participate in the relief efforts. However well-intentioned, the "open for business" phrase signaled a new type of neoliberal economic approach framed and endorsed as a panacea to Haiti's economic ills. In fact, the post-earthquake relief efforts only solidified the "death plan" (which would be later known as the American Plan) a neoliberal economic map designed to decimate the economic lifeline of Haiti (Kennedy and Tilly). This chapter locates the exhibition, "Périféeriques: We are open for Dreaming" curated by Bouchotte, as a response that both critiques the new brand of development masked as economic development and the concept of creative capital, a discursive neoliberal idea maintained through precarity. I begin with a perfunctory history of Caracol to highlight its significance to the country of Haiti, then unravel the theoretical strands

Figure 2.1 Mackenson St-Félix, *Dreams Come True*. Photograph by Josué Azor.

surrounding precarity and situate how Bouchotte's creative production that labors to attest precarity, opens a space that allows for the community of Jacmel to critically interrogate neoliberal economic policies, and dare Haitians to dream of futures (Figure 2.1).

Caracol

The year before the earthquake of 2010, Bill Clinton was named co-chair of a recovery commission which was an international committee functioning under the auspices of the UN to provide relief efforts in Haiti. Coupled with the foundation that bears his name, he hosted foreign companies and banks to persuade them to invest in Haiti. Through his efforts, Clinton garnered the support of international investors to boost tourism, revamp the airport, and construct luxury hotels to make the country more "business friendly." Another aim, particularly that of the recovery commission, was to enhance the manufacturing industry (Bracken; Lall). Clinton, along with the other members of the commission, embraced what is considered a neoliberal approach to economic development. The method promotes international actors such as governments, global corporations, and financial institutions to work in tandem to make conditions (e.g., liberalizing labor laws, tax freedoms, free land) possible for international companies to create export-free zones, which would, in theory, create jobs and thus embolden the local economy (Bracken; Lall). The integration of global economic forces on smaller countries, such as Haiti, has become the new 'development.' A vision of prosperity for Haiti, in the eyes of the Clinton Foundation, the US State Department, and the Inter-American Bank would be international investments in tourism, construction, and low-wage manufacturing jobs (Rodrik). Caracol Industrial Park was designated as an export-free zone for international corporations. The proposal to establish an industrial park was in the planning stages a year before the earthquake of 2010; however, after the catastrophic disaster, the project was expedited.

Located in northern Haiti, just south of the nation's second-largest city Cap Haitian, in the Artibonite region, Caracol is said to have the most fertile land in the country. The large open space that extends from the Kafou Lanmo (the crossroads of death) intersection to the Caracol Bay, holds a distinguished history. Primarily due to previous economic policies imposed by the International Monetary Fund (IMF), brokered under the Clinton presidency, Haiti's agricultural tradition and production are all but devastated, and the country's food system is almost totally reliant on imported goods (Beasley "Women, *Sabotaj*, and Underground Food Economies in Haiti"). Caracol was one of the last remaining areas of independent farm production in the country. The Caracol Bay is also the major source of water for the *Trou du Nor* watershed and an open gateway to other Caribbean Islands. Because of its intact mangroves and coral reefs, it is Haiti's first marine protected area (Steckley and Shamsie; Steckley and Weis). It also houses two critically endangered species: The Atlantic leatherback sea turtle and the black jewfish. Archeologically, the bay is said to be the landing site of the *Santa Maria*, the ship of Christopher Columbus. But the environmental, historical, and contemporary agricultural significance of the Caracol region was ignored when the recovery commission, eager to jump-start Haiti's recovery after the earthquake, quickened efforts and collaborated with the US State Department, the Inter-American Bank, and the international garment company Sae-A to transform the Caracol land to an industrial park to house international manufacturing companies. The slogan of the recovery commission led by Bill Clinton was "building back better." But the building included forcing the movement of 360 families, a construction of a fuel-oil power plant, a dense housing complex and the promise of 20,000 jobs (Sontag). In essence, it was the death of a farming community and culture in one of the last vestiges of such traditional practices in Haiti. The agreement would allow Sae-A, to operate tax-free, have free access to the US market and to provide the workers a wage of 3.75 cents a day, which is far below Haiti's minimum wage.[2] The commission placed more than one-third of the recovery funds in this endeavor as it would be the symbol of Haiti's recovery even though it was in an area unaffected by the earthquake. As of 2017, the park only employs between 8,000 and 9,000 Haitians a small fraction of the 20,000 that was estimated, a profusion of labor violations has been lodged against of Sae-A, and the overall project has had little if any impact on Haiti's economy.[3] The dream of Caracol Industrial Park has not been realized.

Périféeriques against Precarity

At root, precarity is a condition of dependency—as a legal term, precarious describes the situation wherein your tenancy on your land is in someone else's hands. Yet capitalist activity always induces destabilizing scenes of productive destructions— of resources and of lives being made and unmade according to the dictates and whims of the market. But, as David Harvey and many others argue, neoliberal economic practices mobilize this instability in unprecedented ways.

— *Lauren Berlant (2011:192)*

Precarity is a space of unpredictability, instability, and insecurity as Berlant defines above. The term was used with frequency during the 80s. It resurfaced with more attention in the US and Europe during the global recession as economists, sociologists, and even performance theorists, begin to explore more deeply, the domain of the 'precarious' (Ridout and Schneider). Precarity used here refers to portions of society that are reduced to and subjected to flex-ploitation. Existentially, the precariat is a subjugated class that suffers from societal exclusion and even erasure caused by lack of employment, elimination of welfare support systems, and the increasing cost of living. The Occupy movement that began in the United States is an example of how creative and performative actions informed and acknowledged the members of the precariat who were affected by the economic downturn of 2007. The concept of creative capital is not essentially about monetary gain but disseminating destructive political discourses as a means of informing the precariat. Performance theorists have called into question the role of the arts during such fragile economic conditions albeit not to mention call into question the implications of the concept "creative capital." Probing the repositioning of the global economy with the 9/11 as apex as the understanding of the "body" becomes increasingly monetized and emotionally numb. Specifically, how might creative communities along with the global art marketplace conjoin (or not) in questionable economic practices. Pondering the role of representation of others, Butler articulates a concern with the circulation of images in relation to our changing capacity of empathy and interrogates "grievable death" with "livable life" (Butler and Butler). Giscard Bouchotte is familiar with such conversations. He left Haiti to study politics in France and it was there that he witnessed impact of the arts on social and political policy and begin the question the concept of "creative capital." Specifically, the concept as a guise for neoliberal economic policy, particularly in a country like Haiti, a country that lingers in precarity. The interest in art and politics propelled him to curate "Haiti Kingdom of This World" that went to the Venice Biennale and Dak'art, two of the world's leading art fairs. An objective for "Haiti Kingdom of This World" exhibition was to confute current narratives about Haiti. Upon his return to the island, he brought with him the international exhibition to his hometown of Jacmel. He desires to use his curatorial talent to advance social change in Haiti. The political discourse of the international recession, "open for business," had become a much-embraced idiom that functioned as a sign that a particular form capitalism as the panacea for economic ills. Fueled by the energy of the Occupy movement that he witnessed, Bouchotte's use of "creative capital" usurps the political discourse, NGOs, and the international art markets to make the debates surrounding Caracol part of larger intersectional systems about the country of Haiti.

Dreaming

The opening evening was like a cloudy dream of sorts, in the warm and stuffy December evening. As people assemble in the *Place Toussaint Louverture*, the usual open downtown space was invaded with twelve cargo boxes arranged in a semi-circle extending toward twin thoroughfares that converge at the center. As darkness fell and a heavy palpable haze descended from the agitated dust from the nearby roads, the iconic Muybridge "Galloping horse" is projected and scampered across the historic *marché en fer*. Haitian video artist Maksaens Denis mixed the live music and video as dancer Jean-Aurel Maurice, who was wrapped in aluminum foil which blends in and out of the casted blue hues from the projector, weaves in and out of the steel frame (Figure 2.2).

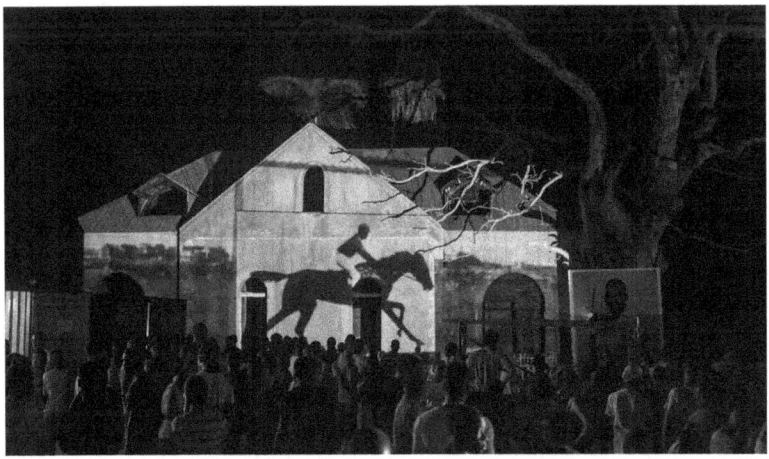

Figure 2.2 Maksaens Denis, *Galloping Horse*. Photograph by Josué Azor.

Denis and Maurice invite the public to a moment of dreaming of possibility as the image of Haiti's distinguished history is projected as the gathered crowd is audibly moved by the splendid visual theater. At moments Maurice's moving body is configured as an angel inviting the onlookers to follow. The interactive performance was a suitable invocation to witness the dreams concealed in the nearby cargo boxes. The public exhibition took place in the municipal center of Jacmel, which is atop a hill overlooking the *Mer Des Antilles*, from December 14 to 29, 2013. The artists who participated were of African-Francophonie descent with significant ties to Haiti, as a place of birth or as a place of residence.

In naming the show, "Périféeriques: We are open for Dreaming," Bouchotte suggested a critical curatorial and political positionality of the identity of Haiti. Périféeriques translated into English means peripheries. Bouchotte rejects a center and margin discourse for a "spatiality of difference" in which individuals situate themselves not in terms of binaries but with the capacity to position self to engage with the margin and center simultaneously (hooks). He alerts both artists and his fellow Haitians that they can intervene "in the face of the arrogance and brutality of the staggering powers of the drifting world." Bouchotte writes in the proposal of the show, "In an 'open for business' country, where the neo-liberal horizon is seen as an unavoidable solution, Périféeriques wants to encourage unexpected initiatives, using different supports and a discourse against the dominant one."[4] The artists set out to consider ways of critically thinking about how social and political policy affect local communities. "We are open for dreaming" seeks to reclaim the physical space of Haiti under threat of international hegemons and appeals to a collective imagination where artists have an important role to work with community. The show is an appeal to expose the problems and to discover new aesthetics, new discourses, and new ways of doing things in a context where the collective interest is rarely considered (Figure 2.3).

In using the object of the cargo box, Bouchotte harkens a history of the port city of Jacmel and the underbelly of globalization. The cargo containers scattered across the landscape of Haiti are repurposed into living spaces, small convenience stores, and I have witnessed one used as a place of worship. In my initial interview with Bouchotte about the use of the cargo boxes, though he acknowledged my statement about the repurposing of the containers, he draws my attention to the plethora of empty storage containers across the landscape of Haiti, including on the beaches of Jacmel. The vacant, abandoned, and desolate objects for Bouchotte

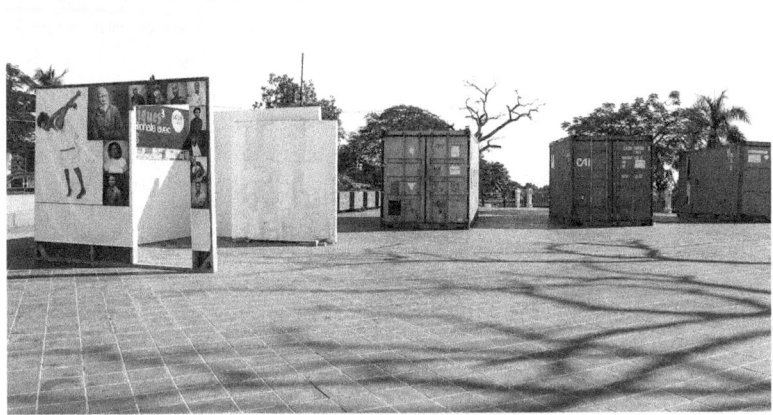

Figure 2.3 Cargoboxes in Jacmel. Photograph by Josué Azor.

connote the precarity of which Haitians might see themselves. Some consider the cargo box, the intermodal transport containers, as principal force behind globalization. Malcolm McLean created a massive system of standardizing shipping containers to make international shipping cheaper. Thus, McLean transformed the transporting of goods around the world. The advancement in the cargo industry devastatingly left many historic port cities (such as Jacmel) abandoned, in favor of newly created docks around the world which provide a greater capacity to import goods and to create tax-free zones (i.e. sweatshops) (Levinson). Though recent efforts exist post-earthquake to revive the historic seaport, the ports of Jacmel have long been abandoned. The cargo boxes Bouchotte situated in the center of Jacmel contains dreams.

Storage of Dreams

The dreams encapsulated in each box, proposed diverse ways of imagining futures. For example, performance artist Joëlle Ferly (Guadelope) installed a video which contained footage of the Digi-cel symbol on various sites throughout Haiti. The rapidly paced footage confronts the ubiquitous nature of the branding of the telecommunication giant on the island. The red and white circular signage stamped on billboards, building, houses, automobiles to rocks, streets, and are found in small far away mountain communities to signal locations of phone charging stations. At one point in the video, Ferly, the artist performs an act of re-branding, in which she paints over the signs with affirming messages about Haiti. Using her body in the video, Ferly warns of our bodies becoming walking brands. The video concludes with question, "Are we Haiti or are we Digicel?" The performative action by Ferly, speaks to individual and collective agency of defining identity. Photographers Antoine Tempé (USA) and Raphael Barontini (France) usurped the historical use of the camera on black bodies and disrupt the mainstream representation of Haiti by allowing Haitians to make their own images. Tempé, recalling the Age'Dor movement of photography of West African of the 1950s, set up his container as a photo studio allowing families, individuals, and groups to a free photo session. While many took this opportunity to get an updated image of themselves and their families, others used the moment to create aspirational portraiture, similar to the images of Samuel Fosso. The photographic studio became a space of performances where participants performed identities before the camera framed in dreams of becoming. Barontini, arrived weeks earlier to capture self-portraits throughout the country. His images were produced into large-scale canvases which were then draped on the exterior of the containers and displayed on buildings and trees throughout the plaza. Tempé and Barontini created spaces for Haitians to see themselves through their own eyes.

Jean-François Boclé (Martinique) sculptured a life size figure out of bananas. The piece titled, *The Tears of Bananaman/Toxic Bananas*, is a response to the recent and rapidly introduction of pesticides to Haiti and other Caribbean Islands. Bolcé draws attention toward the fragility of the countries' food systems. The bananas were inscribed with notations of the dangers of globalization on the agricultural systems of Haiti. As the banana man lay on a small platform, on a screen positioned at the end of the container and above the head of the figure, are images of the messages written on the peel of the bananas. At the revealing of this installation a man in the crowd shouted, "That's a waste of food!" but soon realized after Bouchotte and Bolcé completed their remarks, the audience was expected to consume the bananas. Jacmel is known for its te wouj/red earth. The rich soil made Jacmel a leading site of sugar and coffee production, but because of IMF and the US policies, all major sugar mills have closed, and coffee production currently exists through *ti kiltivatè*, small independent farmers. *The Tears of Bananaman/Toxic Bananas* is a celebratory statement about the natural and abundant resources found on the island, but also the dangers and lethal nature of globalization. I witnessed the performance of a slow death of the banana man as the abundant fruit was consumed throughout the exhibition.

Mackenson St-Félix's (Haïti) installation was aptly titled "Dreams come true." St-Félix placed a box in the center of the container with a sign asking the audience to write their dreams on the small sheet of paper and place them in the box. He explicitly asked for desires, not wishes. Mirrors were situated on three walls of the container for those who wanted to first write their dreams on them as to have them reflected at them. The dreams in the box are to be transformed into reality. St-Félix's installation asked a simple and poignant gesture, but I witnessed how some were confused and could not comprehend what was being asked of them. What does it mean to dream? I stood in front of a man who struggled and kept asking, *"Saw vle di? SA SA vle di ou Reve? Ou vlem ekri rev mwen palew de li?"*/"What do you mean? What do you mean to dream, you want me to write down a dream?" The concept of contemplating a dream is elusive and foreign because of the precarious nature of so many on the island. It was a daunting reality for me to acknowledge and later comprehend the thought of 'dreaming' as a privilege. Yet, Bouchotte astutely and creatively revealed a variety of ways of defining and engaging with dreams/dreaming. "Haiti is for Dreaming" both encourages one to dream and helps define for many in Haiti, to dream and to think of possibility.

The Precious Nature of Things (Haiti Dreamers)

Haiti is predicated on dreams. The effectuation of dreaming of freedom spurred the revolution of the enslaved in 1804. The US military occupation of the 1930s, though resisted by Haiti, demonstrated the island's economic and geographic value, which the French had certainly realized years before.[5] It was the dream of the black nationalists whose rhetoric catapulted a dark skin man from the countryside, Fransçois Duvalier, to the presidency. Yet it was the dream of University of Chicago trained Haitian economist, Leslie Delatour, who served as the Minister of Finance immediately after the ouster of Jean Claude Duvalier, to implement what is known as the "death plan" (which would morph into the "American Plan"). Delatour accelerated a neoliberal economic agenda that, within a matter of two years, privatized the state-owned sugar and flour mills, cement company and rice industries, thus resulting in massive unemployment and leaving Haiti the most privatized and a most precarious nation (Cassen). Reviled by most Haitians, Delatour would be praised by the IMF, World Bank, and the USA. The consistent and constant social protest by the people of Haiti in recent history is testament of how they dream of a better way of life.

What both fascinates and excites me about Bouchotte's project is that it also critiques the international and global art world and demonstrates how the art world, though, perhaps, well-intentioned, in some cases endorse such neoliberal policy (Steckley and Shamsie; Steckley and Weis). In 2009, I was one of the curators of the first Ghetto Biennale that took place in the center of Port-au-Prince at the Grand Rue. A space where international artists came to Haiti to work alongside Haitian artists to produce work. The happening was a critique against the exclusionary practices— both geographic and economic—of the international art market. The event was also a vehicle to provide exposure for Haitian artists whose access to the global market and relations were limited. International artists would come to the event and make lasting relationships and hence, in theory, the unique biennale would forge change. I described the final evening of the fair as a moment of possibility, a temporal suspension of the harsh realities induced an area filled with art and creative production (Beasley "Curatorial Studies on the Edge: The Ghetto Biennale, a Junkyard, and the Performance of Possibility"; Beasley "From Haiti: Gounda Gounda, the Ghetto Biennale and the Performance of Possibility.") The Ghetto Biennale continues today. It has become a brand with the hopes of becoming like other international art fairs that it once claimed to critique. In essence, the organizers are "capitalizing" on the impecunious representation of Haiti. The artists and the community of the Grand Rue, for whom that event was to support, have profited very little if any. The conditions of the neighborhood are worse, not better. The careers of the organizers from outside of Haiti have profited if not monetarily, professionally. The Ghetto Biennale has come to participate in the "poverty chic" discourse rooted in the subjugation and exotification of the other. If the Ghetto Biennale were a critical and emancipatory enterprise, there would not be a need for such an event today. It lingers and can only exist if the Grand Rue community, Haiti, remains in a precarious economic condition. "Haiti is open for Dreamers" proposes meaningful and lasting emancipatory movement. Bouchotte's use and actualization of the term dreaming in the performative actions, rhetorically signifies Haiti's import geographically and underscores the persistent nature of "dreaming" to maintain the revolutionary aspiration.

The situation in Haiti is precarious. I departed Haiti on January 11, 2010, just a day before the devastating earthquake that crippled the country from Port-Au-Prince to the southeastern region of Jacmel. According to the Humanitarian Aid Report 2016, despite the investment in expensive hotels and tax-free zones, the condition of many Haitians continue to be dire. The fragility of Haiti's economic, political, and agricultural structures exists because of external interventions. The mass destruction of the earthquake was worsened because of the privatization of major industries and the elimination of the country's infrastructure put in effect by the death (American) plan designed in the 80s. Clinton has apologized for the decisions made during his administration that crippled the island's agrarian industry. Caracol Industrial Park remains a symbol of neoliberal policies deployed toward Haiti—systems that operationally function to keep Haiti in a precarious state. Bouchotte's "Haiti is for Dreamers" informs the masses of such pernicious policies and challenges his fellow Haitians to dream. "Haiti is for Dreamers" is an action to recall and reclaim Haiti as a precious state.

Notes

1 The quote is from the text printed on the poster for the event, which occurred in November of 2015.
2 Sae-A sew and produce garments for US- based companies such as the Gap, Target, Walmart, and Kohls.
3 The company has a history of labor abuses in their plants in Central America and Southeast Asia, which were reported to the US State Department prior to the groundbreaking.
4 Quote from the exhibition proposal.
5 Haiti was the most valued of the Caribbean colonies. The sugar and coffee from the island were the most valued in the colonial world.

Works Cited

Beasley, Myron M. "Curatorial Studies on the Edge: The Ghetto Biennale, a Junkyard, and the Performance of Possibility." *Journal of Curatorial Studies*, vol. 1, no. 17, 2012, pp. 65–81.
———. "From Haiti: Gounda Gounda, the Ghetto Biennale and the Performance of Possibility." *ElSE: The Journal of Art, Literature, and Philosophy*, 2014, pp. 104–11.
———. "Women, Sabotaj, and Underground Food Economies in Haiti." *Gastronomica*, vol. 12, no. 2, 2012, pp. 33–44, JSTOR, doi:10.1525/gfc.2012.12.2.33.
Berlant, Lauren Gail. *Cruel Optimism*. Duke University Press, 2011.

Bracken, Amy. "Does Haiti Really Need Luxury Hotels?" *Business, Economies and Jobs*. The World https://theworld.org/stories/2013-11-25/does-haiti-really-need-luxury-hotels. Accessed March 24 2022.

Butler, J. and M.E.P.R.J.P. Butler. *Precarious Life: The Powers of Mourning and Violence.* Verso, 2004.

Cassen, Bernard. "Haïti Dans La Spirale Du Désespoir." *Le Monde Diplomatique* https://www.monde-diplomatique.fr/1997/10/CASSEN/4941. Accessed March 24 2022.

Clinton, Hillary Rodham. "Remarks at the Caracol Industrial Park Opening Ceremony." *U.S. Department of State* https://2009-2017.state.gov/secretary/20092013clinton/rm/2012/10/199451.htm. Accessed March 24 2022.

hooks, bell. *Yearning: Race, Gender, and Cultural Politics.* South End Press, 1990.

Kennedy, Marie and Chris Tilly. "Up against the "Death Plan": Haitians Resist Us-Imposed Economic Restructuring." *Dollars & Sense*, Article, 1996, March-April 1996, p. 8+. Gale General OneFile, https://link.gale.com/apps/doc/A18541082/ITOF?u=bates_main&sid=summon&xid=dcd38d522022/3/23/.

Lall, Rashmee Roshan. "An Unlikely Location for Luxury." *Heads Up. New York Times* https://www.nytimes.com/2013/05/26/travel/haiti-an-unlikely-location-for-luxury.html. Accessed March 24 2022.

Levinson, Marc. *The Box: How the Shipping Container Made the World Smaller and the World Economy Bigger.* Princeton University Press, 2016.

Puar, Jasbir. "Precarity Talk: A Virtual Roundtable with Lauren Berlant, Judith Butler, Bojana Cvejić, Isabell Lorey, Jasbir Puar, and Ana Vujanović." *TDR (1988–)*, vol. 56, no. 4, 2012, pp. 163–77, JSTOR, http://www.jstor.org/stable/23362779.

Ridout, Nicholas and Rebecca Schneider. "Precarity and Performance. An Introduction." *TDR: Drama Review*, vol. 56, no. 4, 2012, pp. 5–9, doi:10.1162/DRAM_a_00210.

Rodrik, Dani. "Trading in Illusions." *Foreign Policy*, no. 123, 2001, pp. 54–62, doi:10.2307/3183155.

Sontag, Deborah. "Earthquake Relief Where Haiti Wasn't Broken." *The New York Times* https://www.nytimes.com/2012/07/06/world/americas/earthquake-relief-where-haiti-wasnt-broken.html. Accessed March 24 2022.

Steckley, Marylynn and Yasmine Shamsie. "Manufacturing Corporate Landscapes: The Case of Agrarian Displacement and Food (in)Security in Haiti." *Third World Quarterly*, vol. 36, no. 1, 2015, pp. 179–97, doi:10.1080/01436597.2015.976042.

———— and Tony Weis. "Peasant Balances, Neoliberalism, and the Stunted Growth of Nontraditional Agro-Exports in Haiti." *Canadian Journal of Latin American and Caribbean Studies*, vol. 41, no. 1, 2016, pp. 1–22, doi:10.1080/08263663.2015.1130293.

3 9 of 219/A Carnival of Caskets

Trinidad and Tobago is known for the annual public ceremony of Carnival. It is a mark of commercialism because it is a significant tourist attraction in which the locals plan their year in anticipation. The event functions as both a symbol of the island's national identity and a reminder of its painful history toward black and brown people. The public festival where locals and pilgrims converge on the island to enact folk narratives is a recalling or a hailing of traditions, histories, and religions. Instead of Carnival, many Caribbean islands embrace *En Más* or simply *Mas,* a shortened appellation for the word masquerade. A fitting term for such a public event. The word derives from *mask* as in to pretend and disguise, but I tend to associate the word with concealment as in to cover up or hide. The polyvocal performance of Carnival is public insofar as it carries the ideology of openness. Still, its mere history and even contemporary reading of the ceremony portends acts of erasure as the revelers' parade through streets, each participating in performances that reveal stories, sometimes their story and sometimes others, wrapped in the public narrative. Performance theorist Conquergood reminds us that "cultural performances are not simply epideictic spectacles: investigated historically within their political context they are profoundly deliberative occasions" (Conquergood). The public celebratory events are, in essence, about forgetting.

In 2011, Ebony Patterson arrived in Port of Spain, Trinidad/Tobago. She was one of five artists invited to celebrate the fifth anniversary of the creative and experimental collaborative space, Alice's Yard. This chapter considers Patterson's *9 of 219* performance. She evokes elements of *En Mas* as an innovative intervention that was a direct response to death and violence in Trinidad during the summer of 2011. I position *9 of 219,* a public performance, as a rupture in the discourse of violence surrounding black bodies, not only the "reported" violence to which Patterson

DOI: 10.4324/9780429028489-3

responds directly but epistemological violence that is pervasive in academic research of which neoliberal global policy is often predicated. The *9 of 219* public performance disrupts how the concept of violence should be understood in the context of the Caribbean and the African Diaspora generally. Patterson helps to remind us that discourses of death and violence that surround black bodies are anti-black discourses and how neo-liberal policies, and commercialized public ceremonies create and even sustain such violence. As James writes, "Patterson makes space for an evocative exploration of codes and violence" as entangled in contemporary post-colonial and post-independent diasporic worlds (2012). Patterson's *9 of 219* is a protestation of localized violence that is both transitional and diasporic as she "plays" with the concept of *En Mas* to unmask that which it masked.

Playing with Gender, Violence, and Death

The work of Ebony Patterson is deceptively discomforting. I remember viewing her work for the first time, the aesthetically cushy pictorial blankets of cloth that were variedly quilted and appliqued fabrics of vibrating floral colors, glittering beads, interspersed with artificial flowers, silks and glass, and other found objects. A cursory viewing of Patterson's work might suggest collage. Trained in drawing and printmaking, her earlier noted work, mixed media on paper. *Gangstas for Life* is a series in which she, influenced by dance hall culture, plays with the themes of skin bleaching and hyper-masculinity. The large-scale portraits of men (some from the Most Wanted List, some friends, some famous figures in Jamaica) hand embellished in pastels, glitter, and beads, to critique dancehall culture and play with gender performance and gender inversions. Cloth and other materials continue to be the foundational canvas of her work. I worked with Patterson in 2009 in Haiti, where she began to incorporate the use of fabric and other material objects to the work influenced by her collaborations with Haitian Confectionneur de Drapeaux vodou. Vodou Flags are skillfully beaded textile objects dedicated to a *Lwa* and used in sacred ceremonies. Often adorning the walls of peristyles (voodoo worship centers) and in personal spaces of devotees, they are also considered precious and valuable art objects. Patterson's installation in Haiti included four large Vodou Flags, in which she recontextualized images of young Jamaican men as Vodou *Lwa.* Building on the dancehall bling aesthetic and Haitian Vodou, the project played with gender fluidity in the representation of the *Lwa*. The installation also included detailed offerings as a shrine to the sacred spirits of Vodou. The work in Haiti, according to Patterson, was a turning point in her work.

The 2018 exhibition, "*…. while the dew is still on the roses…*," at the Perez Art Museum was a massive endeavor. The installation incorporated videos, photography, sculpture, and other various medium representing her body of work over ten years with new work. The walls coated with fabric textured wallpaper with the bling'd artifacts smothering the floor. The title is from the Christian hymn, *In the Garden*, known mainly by its first line, *I come to the garden alone*, written by American songwriter C. Austin Miles. Patterson describes the installation as a night garden as the audience perambulates through the exquisitely designed plots and survey but then scrutinize to succumb that the garden is a graveyard. Miles's song is a requiem as Patterson's installation is a memorial to the dead. The work is seductively dangerous as it entices with the sparkle and the bling yet reveals the violence inflicted on black bodies.

The Jamaican artist uses the traditional dancehall aesthetic meshed with pop culture, engages with questions surrounding gender performativity, disrupts binaries, evocatively challenges colorism, and acknowledges the prevalence of violence that leads to the death of black bodies. The alluring beauty of Patterson's work; the layering, complicated, and the nuanced aesthetic forces a careful scopic examination—the previous work including *Dead Treez* (2015), a solo exhibition for the Museum of Arts and Design. Moreover, in "*… bearing witness …*" (2017), Patterson continues to take up the topic of the perpetual violence against the black body. Specifically, she attends to the replaying and circularity of repeated enactments of brutality in public spaces as reperformed on social media platforms.

The Parade of Caskets

"I arrived with nothing, no preconceived project; I was taking a risk as an artist," Patterson comments about her arrival in Port of Spain in the summer of 2011 (Figure 3.1). She had not come with a precise plan for her creative venture. It was an expectation that each artist would conclude their residency with an exhibition. Upon her arrival, Patterson's brief tour of the island concludes at a bead shop. At the store, Patterson was taken by the expression of empathy displayed by the store owner. The owner who viscerally responded

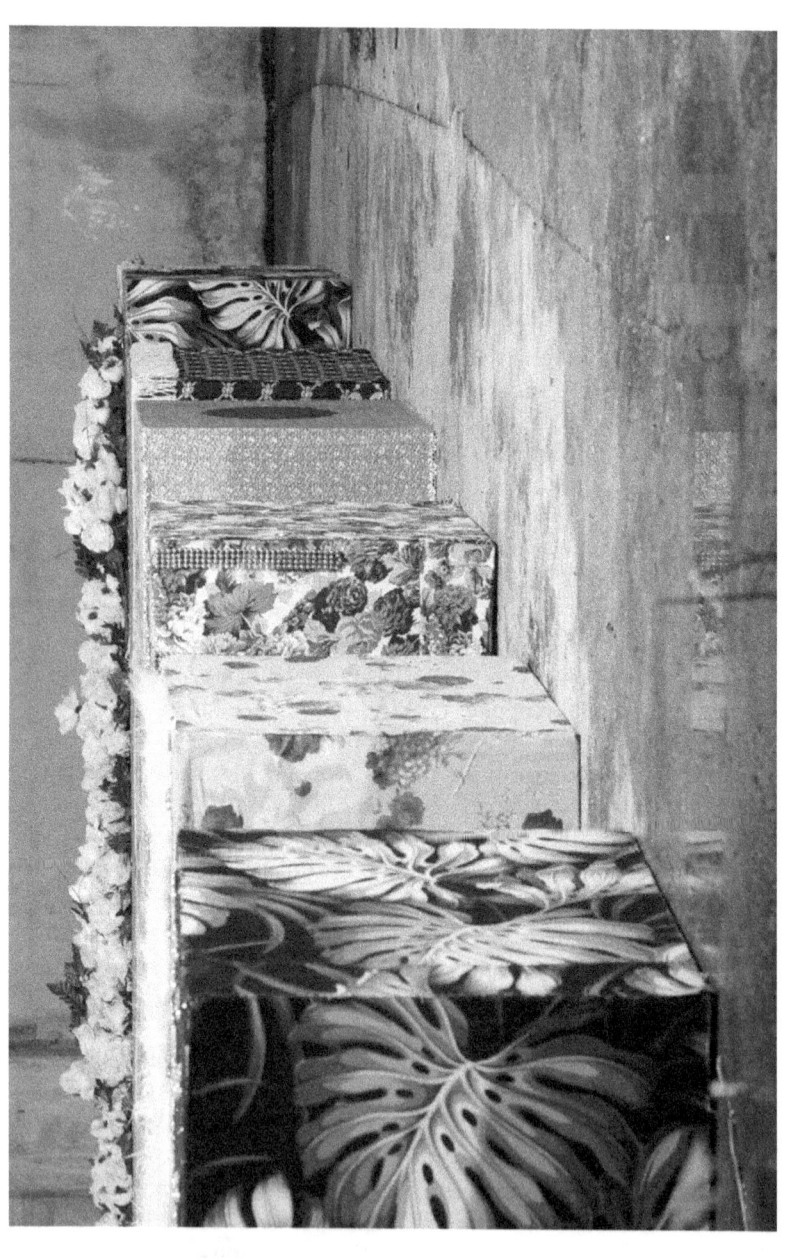

Figure 3.1 Photo by Rodell Warner, Courtesy of Ebony G. Patterson and Monique Meloche Gallery.

to the announcement of another murder broadcasted on the radio that played in the background. "The store owner was so expressive that I assumed that the person mentioned was a personal friend of hers, but it wasn't" Patterson shared. However, she did not. "It was a common reaction, I discovered, a genuine concern regarding the state of crime," Patterson claims she witnessed, "people stop and listen to the obituaries and then make commentary about the loss of the individual." She continues, "everyone stopped and listened. It gave her pause because, "being from Jamaica, I realized that I was desensitized to the announcements of murders."

It was that and other similar interactions that inspired *9 of 219*. Patterson decided to record all the murders of the first week and stage a funeral performance. The objective was to make one coffin a day for every murder committed during her first week and a half. For nine days, she would scour the newspaper looking for obituary announcements. She waited, "Just imagine it was a long process of waiting and checking, hoping and not hoping, it's kinda weird, waiting for somebody to die to make an art project, at the same time that nobody dies that you don't have to make an art project." After the waiting period, Patterson constructed nine simple wooden coffins that were then "blinged" in with tapestry, beads, and glitter for which she is known. Each coffin was unique and reflected the social and cultural contours of the location.

On the night of the announced "opening" at Alice's Yard, people arrived expecting to attend a traditional gallery opening. Instead, Patterson, who collaborated with the rapso group 3Canal, invited the audience to take a coffin (four people per coffin) and march through the city. The parade would be accompanied by 3Canal playing *Pita Pata* (Manwarren 4:11) with the reading of the obituaries of the murdered a loud. Significant to the oral performance of the eulogies was the description of each person, thus personalizing the dead. Seven of the nine coffins were carried in the procession as some audience members refused to participate. Alas, along the funeral procession lasting just over an hour, the parade was halted twice—first, by a police officer. Patterson insisted that the performance was an art project. The police stated that there were complaints, not of loud music, but of a woman carrying a coffin. The second interruption was from the police chief, who stopped them and questioned if they had a permit for the performance and warned them to stay in the yard. The audience returned to the art center, and the caskets were placed in the yard with candles illuminating the art center.

Archaeologies of Violence and the Carnivalesque

According to Thomas, "violence destroys, but also generates divergent ways of community and citizenship." Necropolitics are deliberatively constructed systems that function to annihilate (Mbembe and Corcoran). With the advent and the dispersal of black bodies in the trans-Atlantic slave trade, violence was perpetrated on the enslaved by imperial settlers. The deployment of violence worked to consolidate empire and nationalism in Europe and to inculcate terror to the enslaved. Through my dwelling and working in various locations of the African Diaspora, I have learned that to grasp, to comprehend, to describe, and even to define the concept of violence is to embrace the fluid and shifting surges of religion, politics, economics, labor, and popular culture with temporalities and geographies. The comprehension of violence in the context of the African Diaspora is complex. As I claimed earlier in this text, art and performance have the immense capacity to "theorize" and "make sense" of social issues in ways that cut across various discursive formations. Patterson, in *9 of 219*, from the intricate details of the caskets and the use of rapso music, captures the complexities of lived realities inclusive of time, history, religions, and folklore. A palimpsest comes to mind—a word I often use as a metaphor to consider the unraveling of thought but also the persistent lingering of what has come before. The engraved imprints of that thought to be erased seeps through as a penumbra of history. The tracks and traces of discourses inscribed on spaces and bodies each layer reveal elements of what was before. One could consider the Caribbean islands generally as a palimpsest. What Benítez-Rojo (1996) suggests as palimpsestic time, I consider hauntology of performance (Moten; Muñoz) implying that the discursive enactments never end but rather participate in a dialect shifting and bending with the unsettling and oppressive discourses as they emerge again and again. Here, I situate and read the *9 of 219* performance as carnival.

As a public cultural performance, Carnival in Trinidad and Tobago is a sign of commercialism and tourism for which the island is known. Yet, it is a public memorial that signals a colonial past. As I read the *9 of 219* performance as carnival, it opens up a space to interrogate both the cultural and systematic structures of violence and encourages a discussion of the essence of Fanon's work, the per-durable efficacy of internalized racism. Yet, as I return to Mbembe and ponder necropolitics as purposefully designed apparatus that function to annihilate, I consider the contribution of academic research, the academy, in the creation and sustaining of execrable policies. What follows is a palimpsestic reading of the Patterson's *9 of 219* performance that weaves folkloric and cultural perfor-mances with history, religion, and politics ultimately to peel back multiple levels of violence and revealing how Patterson performs a rupture in the discourse.

The concept of *En Mas*, if anything, is a collaborative and com-munal creative production. The annual pageant incorporates vari-ous creative elements from the visual arts, costumes, music, dance, and even theatricality. Yet on one level, it is easy for me to consider Gilroy and his theoretical treatise in which he proposes a differ-ent way of examining the Black Atlantic diasporic routes to sug-gest how forced migration caused, "syncretic pattern in which the styles and forms of the Caribbean, the United States, and African have been reworked and reinscribed in the novel context of modern Britain's own untidy ensemble of regional and class-oriented con-flicts" (Gilroy). And the formative work of Roach, who asks us to consider a lens toward a circum-Atlantic performance which is an energetic convergence and "behavioral vortex where cultural trans-mission may be detoured, deflected, or displaced" (Roach). Both theorists proffer distinctive methods of deciphering and reading the residue of the trans-Atlantic flows of knowledge and culture. In 2014, Claire Tancons curated a year-long, multi-site exhibition titled *En Mas': Carnival and Performance Art of the Caribbean*. The project highlighted the creative productions of Carnival and its rela-tion to the European avant-garde. Specifically, *En Mas'* is a critical response to art history and challenges the genealogies of perfor-mance art, signaling that the concept of Carnival, particularly in ways in which it has been performed throughout the years, should be considered the initiators of the Avant-Garde before—the Euro-peans. But more importantly and significant, for this project, Tan-cons advocates a decentering of the concept of Carnival to reflect the epistemological and ontological shifts of the parades to locals in the Caribbean. To understand Carnival in its multiple meanings, it is essential to take up the regional interpretations and performances to de-masquerade all that the parade seeks to mask and conceal. Reading the Patterson's *9 of 219* is an un-masking to bring attention to death and violence on the island.

Genealogies of Violence

In one of our conversations about the project and violence in Trinidad and Tobago, Patterson claimed that she was numb to violence because "I'm from Jamaica." That admission suggests that she has experienced or witnessed a type of physical violence living on the island, and she could speak to that claim, or rather, she has come to believe, the national and international discourse deployed that Jamaica is a violent country. That summer, while Patterson was in residence at Alice's Yard, according to international governmental reports, like those issued from the United States State Department, from 2009 and onto 2011, Trinidad Tobago was cited as having the largest murders per capita in the Caribbean (Hohnholz). The *9 of 219* performance is a response to physical, mental, and even economic violence. Both products of colonialism are complex in that they feed into one another. Patterson tapped into the global political shifts beginning after World War 1 and exploded in the 60s, which brought about the struggle for the independence of colonized nation-states in full force.

In such cases, the imperialists left little if any economic structures in place, but what they did leave behind was Western notions of gender, sexual norms, and hierarchies of class strata which was intertwined with how to be a good citizen. The Western cultural imprints would be reinforced by global financial institutions such as the World Bank and the International Monetary Fund. The discourse of black families as dysfunctional and deficient began to gain circulary in tandem with the discourse of violence. Thomas (2011) provides an exhaustive treatment of quantitative analytical and historical research and outlines how faulty and questionable methods, and analyses are used by NGOs and other aid and development organizations. The erroneous data and research compiled by academics continue to be used as a baseline for international government systems to provide structural monetary relief in this post-colonial moment. The structural adjustment policies tie developmental funding to Western cultural ideas such as "population control" (forced sex education, birth control experimentation) and home economics (instructions in schools and trades to codify Western gender roles and the definition of family). More perplexing, the "forced" norms were tied to the concept of citizenship. To be a civilized and a good citizen was to master, or to be like the colonist in ways of speaking, dressing, education, etc. Thus, the tactics used by International Monetary Fund and other global economic organizations as an attempt to foster economic sustainability post-independence is nothing more than a continuation of colonialism. Fanon is preoccupied with the question, what does it mean to disrupt the internalized thinking that your black body is not worthy, intellectually inferior, and not beautiful (Fanon)? Patterson's comment about being numb to the violence and her performance echoes persistent struggle of internalization of people of African descent. Fanon addresses the colonized intellectual as one who also perpetuates the oppressive systems that degrade even themselves because their mere training is steep in the repressive way of thinking, and it reinforces a colonial positionality. This form of violence is epistemological, which casts doubt on different knowledge systems from the subjugators. The type of violence I speak here is masked in academic liberalism from those who do culturally based work. We tend to seek the "traditional" African variable to claim its legitimacy and cultural production. I have struggled to think of Patterson's performance through my writing and thinking of art and performance more generally in a language and articulation that best reveal a different optic, a different way of thinking other than my European trained reading of creative cultural productions. It is a different type of intellectual labor to produce "scholarship" that will look unique, sound unfamiliar and ask the reader to push beyond the boundaries of their understanding of the world. It also challenges me to stretch outside my Western training limitation to endeavor discomfort and vulnerability while not deploying epistemological violence. Critics such as Tancons and Thompson move to write toward a different type of art criticism and artist writing, particularly regarding Caribbean cultural production.

Patterson's project works across temporalities, history, and culture to disrupt and reveal systems that perpetuate death and violence. The walk, the promenade through the city, is one such example of how she employs specific cultural references which acknowledge the rich cultural history of the island and the disturbing contemporary realities. The walk, as echoed by de Certeau, can be a form of activism. For Peterson to lead participants to march through Port of Spain's streets is to unmask and untangle the narratives of death and violence about the cityscape, it is to write a new, to make known the unseen. The strolling orchestrated by Patterson at the opening represents one narrative, which is crisscrossed with the oral reading of the obituaries and 3Canal's performance of "Pita Pita."

The use of music, but specifically rapso music, recalls a history of protest. Calypso music is central to *Mas* in Port of Spain. Calypso bands compete throughout the carnival celebration. A style of music developed in Trinidad during the 17th century, calypso comes from protest. Specifically, songs led by a griot or calypsonian, in a call and response performance, where the enslaved on the plantations would mock the plantation owners. It was a provocative way in which the enslaved would communicate with each other, and more importantly, it is a vehicle to disseminate information. Contemporary calypso songs tend to address political issues and politicians. Rapso is a genre derived from Calypso that emerged from the Union and Black Power movements of the 1960s. It is often characterized as and equated with American "Rap" music. Not only does Patterson deploys rapso music, but she also garners support from the popular band, thus connecting a tradition of the past with the present. The song selected is 3Canal's song "Pita, Pata" (Manwarren 4:11). The song's lyrics are both a wake-up call to the living and a requiem to the dead.

"This place have too much ah guns!" then it moves to the refrain: "Pita pata, piti pata" to evoke the sound of gun shots. "Awake, arise from your sleep and slumber/Arise 'cause our days are numbered'/ Woe be unto them sleepwalking in this time of reckoning/Yeah, though I walk through the shadows in the valley/I shall far no evil one/" (Manwarren 4:11).

As a call to action, the song asks the community to wake up to see what is happening. The call is to "... awake, arise from your sleep and slumber ..." because "You can't be afraid in your own land" then asks, "Can you tell me what's the matter? /Pita pata, pita, pata. This place have too much ah guns! ... open up your eyes!" (Manwarren 4:11) The group sounds the alarm to the violence and rampant availability of guns on the island. Yet as a requiem, the song evokes biblical references associated with death. For example, one line, "Yeah, though I walk through the shadows in the valley/I shall fear no evil one/For they rod, and staff are with me" (Manwarren 4:11). The walk, as mentioned above—a walk through the valley, is to suggest the island is the valley. But do not fear. Interestingly the biblical reference to Psalm 23 is about life as it is about death. It affirms to the living that to walk through the valley is to acknowledge and to know the city and perhaps then to know thy, neighbor. Maybe then to sincerely get to know is to engage fully and recognize the neighbor would prevent violence. It is a call to humanity. The decorative blinged caskets deploy another level of representation of death.

When the first police officers arrive, they claim that a person called the police station and complained of a woman walking around with a casket. In Trinidadian folklore character, the Lagahoo is a shapeshifting being. During the day, they embody the essence of a human, but in the evening, they roam about headless with a wooden casket chained to their necks. The coffins are topped with three lit candles. A powerful being that is both feared and respected, the Lagahoo possesses the power to transform into various animals, as well as curse and heal, and protect. He also can facilitate a transition to death. Folklore, according to Gencarella (2009) "... is not something that a folk does; rather, it is something that, in its doing, constitutes a folk" (173). Myths of the Caribbean can be traced to the African diasporic religious belief systems and are intertwined with what Roach labels as the circum-Atlantic performance. They embrace a dynamic and non-linear conception of thinking about the transference of cultural production at every level from the local to the global. Folklore, as a set of aesthetic expressions that moves diasporically, relays truths about a culture and people.

Patterson cleverly performs a disruption in the city of Port of Spain. The *9 of 219* performance reveals multiple layers of systems, particularly in the Caribbean, that precipitate death and violence. The performance, in many ways, functions as an anti-Mas in that it functioned to unmask as to ask the community to ponder its history with the colonial present. From the caskets to the use of rapso, 9 of 219 asks the public to consider the meaning and purpose of cultural production and bring to the fore that which is often forgotten—or erased—to evoke communities to look and examine the political structures that function to annihilate. A parade through the city is never just a parade.

Works Cited

Benítez Rojo, Antonio and James E. Maraniss. *The Repeating Island: The Caribbean and the Postmodern Perspective.* Second ed., Duke University Press, 1996. vol. Book, Whole.

Certeau, Michel de. *The Practice of Everyday Life.* University of California Press, 1984. vol. Book, Whole.

Conquergood, Dwight. "Rethinking Ethnography: Towards a Critical Cultural Politics." *Communication Monographs*, vol. 58, 1991, pp. 179–94, http://www.csun.edu/~vcspc00g/603/RethinkingEthnography-DC.pdf.

Fanon, Frantz. *The Wretched of the Earth.* First evergreen ed., Grove Press, 1966. vol. Book, Whole.

———— and H. Chevalier. *A Dying Colonialism.* Grove Press, 1994.

Gencarella, Stephen Olbrys. "Constituting Folklore: A Case for Critical Folklore Studies." *The Journal of American Folklore,* vol. 122, no. 484, 2009, pp. 172–96, doi:10.1353/jaf.0.0086.

Gilroy, Paul. *The Black Atlantic: Modernity and Double Consciousness.* Harvard University Press, 1993. vol. Book, Whole.

Hohnholz, Linda. "Trinidad & Tobago Now Murder Capital of the Caribbean." *Global Travel Industry News* https://eturbonews.com/19238/trinidad-tobago-now-murder-capital-caribbean/. Accessed March 24 2022.

Manwarren, Wendell, et al. "Piti Pata." *Spotify* https://open.spotify.com/track/728Qrri8WMHw6ckkd76jAR?si=ZIVQhLDmSLKeLGpZm RFqVA&nd=1. 2005.

Mbembe, Achille and Steve Corcoran. *Necropolitics.* Duke University Press, 2019. vol. Book, Whole.

Moten, Fred. *In the Break: The Aesthetics of the Black Radical Tradition.* N - New ed., University of Minnesota Press, 2003. vol. Book, Whole.

Muñoz, José Esteban. *Disidentifications: Queers of Color and the Performance of Politics.* vol. 2., University of Minnesota Press, 1999. vol. Book, Whole.

Roach, Joseph. *Cities of the Dead: Circum-Atlantic Performance.* Columbia University Press, 2021. vol. Book, Whole.

Thomas, D.A. *Exceptional Violence: Embodied Citizenship in Transnational Jamaica.* Duke University Press, 2011.

4 Public Mourning/ Performance as Life

I am first of all an artist but because the literal meaning of an activ-ist is someone who is working towards achieving social and political change, I will accept it if you call me one. However, when you look at this deeply, I am just an artist. The function of an artist is to activate the environment but if I try to activate mine and you call it activism, then I would disagree with you. I am trying to be a pure artist who does not feel that I should use my talent to earn money just for myself, rather it is for me to enhance the consciousness of my audience.

—Jellili Atiku, Omenka Gallery

Jelili Atiku responds to social topics with public performances in the middle of town squares, through the streets of rural neighbor-hoods, and inside legislative buildings (Figure 4.1). The interna-tionally recognized multimedia performance artist was awarded the coveted Prince Claus Award in 2015. Despite Atiku's highlight-ing human rights and social justice issues in his practice, he was selected to represent Nigeria in the 2017 Venice Biennale. He contin-ues to live in his home community of Ejigbo outside the metropolis of Lagos, where many neighbors are unaware of his international reputation. The Yorùbá faith which informs Atiku's understanding of death and politics, is what motivates him to use his talent to fight for social justice and human rights concerns and to labor toward decolonizing himself and others (Tewa).

The domain of performance art is the sometimes-indecipherable line between life and art. It is that characteristic of performance art that makes it powerful and dangerous. Atiku has mastered the ability to make his work communally engaged in various contexts around the world, and because of his Yorùbá faith, his artmaking for him is spiritual and sacred (Tewa). This chapter culminates with the examination of the performance *Aragamago, We Rid This*

DOI: 10.4324/9780429028489-4

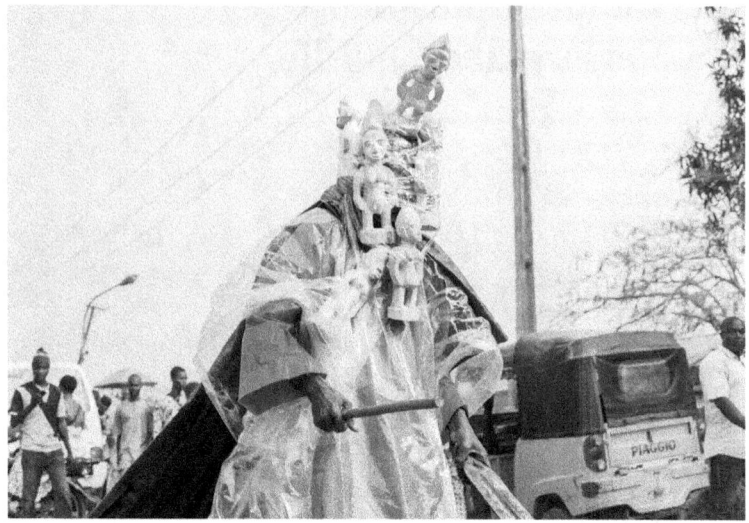

Figure 4.1 Image by Emmanuel Sanni from the Collection of Jelili Atiku.

Land Off Terrorism, Atiku's response to an event in his community in Nigeria, and the interrogation of the Yorùbá faith that complicates the meaning of performance art and activism with the sacred and the secular. "My reason for performance art is as a result of my quest for self-decolonization," says Atiku, who fully embraces the Africana philosophy of Yorùbá.[1] He insists his movement to critique political issues of his home country of Nigeria and inter nationally are fueled by his transition to understanding and rediscovering his indigenous background and beliefs. His work critiques political systems and aims to decolonize culture and western constructs of art and education. Atiku's embrace and celebration of Yorùbá is a form of resistance against necropolitical regimes of power and discourses.

Visceral and Virtual

Mbembe's thoughts of necropolitics are both a critique and a rethinking of Foucault's biopolitics. Specifically, Mbembe considers Foucault's understanding of the body as a vehicle of production. The premise suggests that capitalist systems promote docility through an abstractive view of corporeality that is reinforced by the church, education, and medical establishments. The body is created to labor, to produce, not to think. But the concept of death here is expansive and concerns itself with the visceral and virtual dialectic. The concept of the simulacra, the inability to distinguish reality from the virtual, is a strategy used to obscure both our perceptions of and the real tangible yearnings and feeling of our physical bodies. Mbembe argues that because of the obsession with quantification of human experience and entanglement with social media, we disregard the physical bodily experiences for a mediated (fake) world. Reasoning,

> ...turns into a mathematical object, it becomes urgent to oppose an epistemic hegemony that reduces the Earth to a financial problem and a problem of financial value...Were data to overcode the subject, to act without reasoning to leave behind reflexive thinking, and to privilege data correlation, then formal language and inferential deductions would become the norm. The computation age (the age of Facebook, Instagram, Twitter) is dominated by the idea that there are clean slates in the unconscious.
>
> (Mbembe 113–14)

Technological advances work to separate the emotive bodily experience from mediated representations of the body. It advances docility, thus enabling the citizenry to be easily persuaded to promote discourse and policies against themselves and others. "The body itself is neither power nor value. Rather its power and value result from a process of abstraction based on the desire for eternity" (Mbembe 89). Reason, as he puts it, is promulgated by the church and functions in tandem with political systems to subjugate. The body is understood to labor tirelessly (for capitalism) to death with a promise to achieve eternity. The abstraction is the glorification of labor at the expense of ignoring the body. Denying the body, coupled with the entanglement of mediated realities, makes it easier to will to death the less desirable and participate in the production of one's death. However, the body is configured differently in the Yorùbá faith and presents a radical departure from that espoused by Foucault and Mbembe.

Yorùbá is a complex cosmology with a panoply of orishas that serve as intermediaries between the living (*iye*) and the spiritual world (Drewal). It is the indigenous religion of Yorùbáland, which is the name of the geographic area that is currently the southwestern portion of Nigeria, Benin, and Togo, prior to colonization. It is also an ethnic group. Yorùbá values human connection with nature and holds that individuals possess "Ayanmo"—agency to determine one's fate (Drewal). However, power is situated in the concept of "Àṣẹ," which is the energy found in all of nature. Àṣẹ is both a verbal articulation and physical embodiment of being situated in the here and now. The concept of death (*iku*), like performance, is ephemeral. In Yorùbá, death is a transitionary—a separation of the soul from the body—a process of life to a restorative or renewed energy. Simply, it is not an end or a chasing after eternity but an engagement of a different apparition of being. The body, in the manifestation of the physical world and its connections to nature, has the power to transform. Atiku is motivated by and strongly feels that epistemologically, the premise of Yorùbá is performance:

> During the colonial period, our art suffered many setbacks. For example, performance art is the most ancient and prominent practice in Yorùbáland and of course in Africa but when the British came, they changed several things about us. Looking at the Egungun (masquerade) for example, you may notice that the sculptor creates colorful costumes imbedding several meanings, as well as incorporating poetry and dance. For me, this is art in complete form.[2]

I was introduced to Atiku when I witnessed one installment of his *Araferaku* performance trilogy. The title comes from the Yorùbá language and means, "A part of me is missing." I consider the piece a requiem to his father, who died months before his birth. According to Atiku, the forty-four-hour (reflecting the age of his father at his death) durational meditation "triggers personal emotions with manifest as a eulogy of a son of a father who died seven months before his birth" (Museum Publicity Editors). Happening over the span of three days, the emotionally suffused action begins in a gallery space and processes through the town and concludes in Atiku's neighborhood. The gallery walls were adorned, floor to ceiling, with wallpaper of the only faded image of his father. He moves about attending to a life-size papier-mâché sculpture that looks like a mummified body lying on a thin mattress. After gingerly touching and rubbing the body, he summons his mother to sit next to him on the floor of the gallery. After serving water to her, the mummy, and himself, he then proceeds to bound them

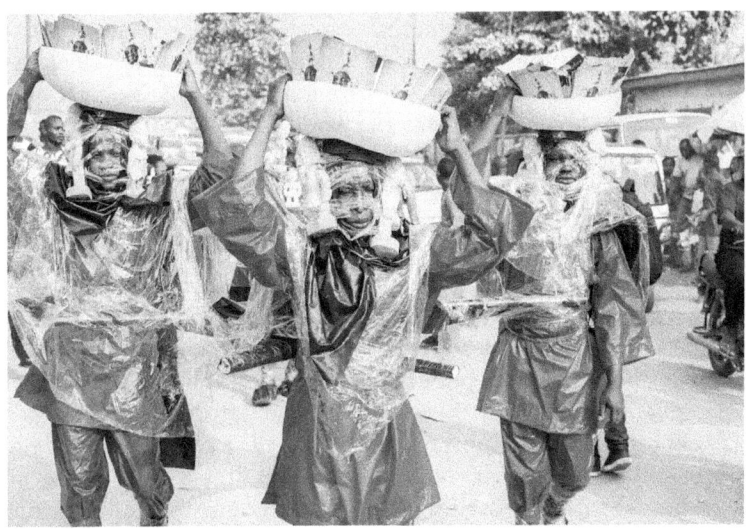

Figure 4.2 Image by Emmanuel Sanni from the Collection of Jelili Atiku.

by wrapping the three of them with yarn as they sit on the floor surrounded by messages to his deceased father scribbled in brown paint. Later the performance moves to his Ejigbo neighborhood. Atiku leads the witnesses from the gallery forming a funeral procession through the metropolis of Lagos his neighborhood. In full ritual attire, made with custom-made fabric with the images of his father printed, the performance took on the feel of a natural memorial to the dead (Figure 4.2).

The power and use of language and words imbue Atiku to Yorùbá because language itself is energy that strengthens and activates the body. By commencing the Araferaku performance in the gallery and moving it out to the streets, Atiku illustrates that there is no difference between the sacred and the secular. The "white walls" of the gallery disappear to realize the beautiful art of everyday existence in nature and life. The sacred is found in daily existence. "A pure artist who does not feel that I should use my talent to earn money," Atiku, responds to a journalist, "rather, it is for me to enhance the consciousness of my audience" (Tewa). His comment to the journalist about being an activist is rejected because, for him, the artist is a shaman, and his creative endeavors are motivated by his connection to nature and Àṣẹ. That impulse, or in his words, activation, fuels his performative responses to social injustice and human rights issues. He is prolific and attends to issues such as the effects of oil exploration in Africa and climate change. In *Come Let Me Clutch Thee*, he likens the world's addiction to oil to "the form of marriage …. marriage with science, of marriage with capitalism, of marriage with the environment, with those who want to explore, who comes with the pretense of amicable relationship that they turn into destruction."[3] Adorned in a white wedding dress, throughout the performance, the partner pours black oil on his body as he perambulates around and through the gallery as the lubricant dribbles off his body, ruining the earth and the floor of the gallery. He publicly challenged and brought attention to a bill quietly making its way through the state legislator to legalize child marriages. Appropriately titled, *The Senator's Wedding*, Atiku pulls a cart with a young girl in a cage dressed in a "western" wedding gown. Purposefully strolling through streets fallen into disrepair, Atiku signals that the politicians should concern themselves with "infrastructure which they don't talk about, and they were talking about having a marriage with a young girl."[3] The use of the "western" wedding dress is to "bring out the foreign idea that is completely alien into our values … they are ideas that have come with colonization. The Yorùbá faith does not support such a practice. It's against our traditions."[4] The public performance of his work buts up against colonial sensibilities, specifically western legal and cultural practices that he would argue is not natural. His performances, widely documented on the internet, are thoughtful, often community-engaged, aesthetically alluring, reflective, and situated in the Yorùbá faith.

Aragamago, We Rid this Land Off Terrorism

On January 18, 2016, three women were arrested at the Market Sodom in Ejigbo for allegedly stealing fifty Naira (which is ten cents, USD) worth of peppers. The women were publicly stripped naked, tortured, and sexually assaulted by ten men who were later identified as security guards. One of the women died as a result of the assault (Figure 4.3). A video of the incident went viral three weeks after the actual assault; the community response was swift with protest, taking to the streets and shouting, "Justice for the Ejigbo 3," demanding the culprits' arrests. According to Atiku, "it

is a taboo to put a woman into a state like that, an inhuman state."[5]
The men who perpetrated the act had not been found or arrested.
Atiku's response to the dehumanizing treatment of three women
was a public performance titled, *Aragamago, We Rid This Land
Off Terrorism,* staged in the streets of his hometown, Ejigbo.
Disappointed by the treatment of the women and as president
of the Ejigbo Indigenous Forum, Atiku demanded a meeting with
the King to address the community's concerns, what he labeled
as "domestic terrorism" by police officers and political lawmak-
ers. When the King denied his request, Atiku created *Aragamago,
We Rid This Land Off Terrorism.* The title is the name of a sacred
bird representing the feminine power of healing.[6] Atiku drafted a
Ìwúre/Ọfọ̀. Earlier, I explained the primacy of language and words
in Yorùbá. The Ìwúre/Ọfọ̀ is a sacred text/object. Ìwúre is the object
that contains and reminds us of the power of words. The Ọfọ̀ are the
incantations, prays, poems, songs the text— the words—that can
be a supplicatory blessing or a curse. Atiku drafted an Ọfọ̀ that was
stridently political, addressing recent events and requesting that the
King demand respect for the rule of law. The document includes a
poem requesting the lives of those who committed the transgres-
sions upon the women would come to a disastrous end. The Ìwúre/
Ọfọ̀ concludes with the term, Àṣẹ, the expression of declaration and
urgency. He printed 15,000 of the Ìwúre/Ọfọ̀, which took the form
of a flyer (Figure 4.3).
    Atiku and his neighbors don red and black plastic sheets as
clothing with small statues of Èrè Ìbejì wrapped around their faces
and heads. The colors black and red are the colors of the Òrìṣà,
Èṣù who is the deity of law enforcement and orderliness. Èṣù is the
chief enforcer of divine and natural laws. The costumes generated
sweat from the bodies of the performers, which in the Yorùbá context, "bring[s] energy of sacred water," as Atiku and his colleagues
walked through the town distributing the Ìwúre/Ọfọ̀ flyers that they
carried on their heads in Igbá Pàkátà (calabash bowls).[7]
    On January 18, 2016, the performance drew the attention of the
King and politicians, who moved to have Atiku, and his colleagues
arrested. In his own words:

    And though the king felt so uncomfortable with that, he called
    the police and they got me and five other people arrested, where
    immediately I was arrested, I was put into police detention
    overnight, so the following morning, they took us to court,

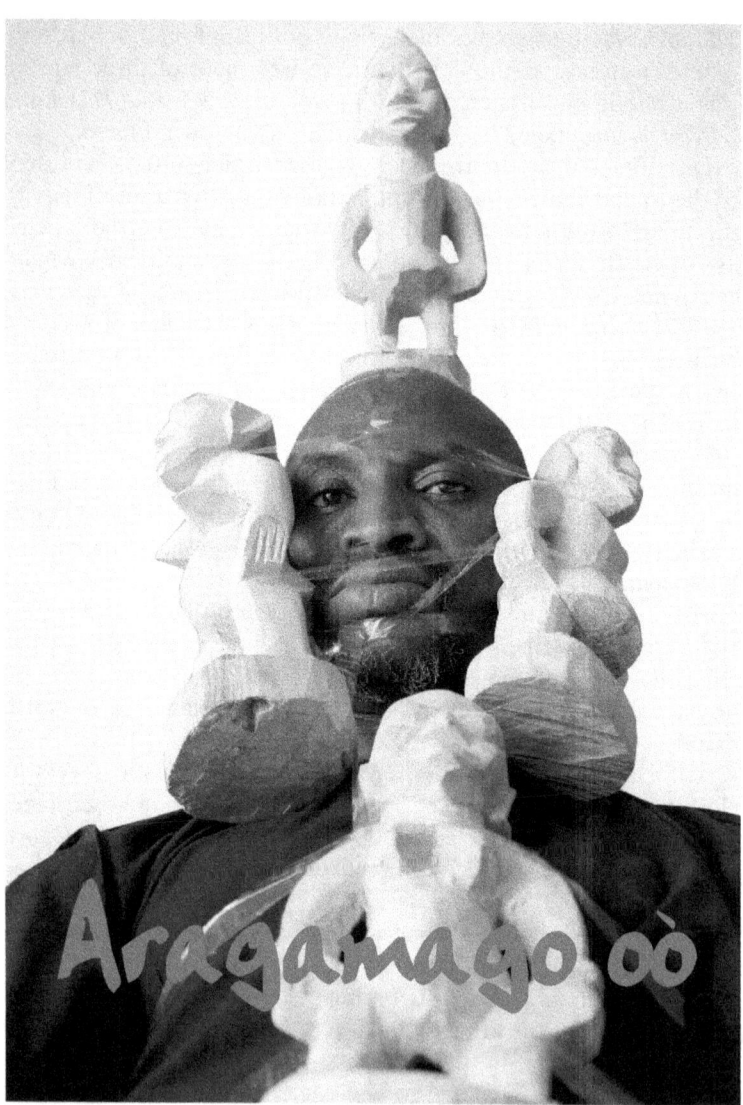

Figure 4.3 Object of Jelili Atiku's Performance, Aragamago Will Rid This
       Land Off Terrorism, at Ejigbo, Lagos on Thursday, January
       14, 2016.

OLÓDÙMARÈ oò
Àṣe ÒRÌS̩À lénu mi oò
Rid our world off TERRORISM o
Eeh! More than 140,000 Terrorists' attacks have occurred worldwide
With records of over 150,000 fatalities
With ceaseless attacks and causalities o:
http://www.freedomnewspaper.com/gambia-breaking-news-isis-
massacred-over-300-west-african-migrants-in-libya-on-new-years-day-
gambian-migrants-account-for-the-chunk-of-those-killed/

Igba IRÚNMO LÈ oò
Clean Ejigbo from DOMESTIC TERRORISM and IMPUNITY oò
These began in December 12 1998.

Kutukutu, Priest of the Dawn oò
In 1999 you know how our elders in Ejigbo were beaten mercilessly
A re-occurrence of such ugly event happened again on February 18 2001
Several properties were destroyed, many sustained severe injuries
And many died.

Ganrin ganrin, Priest of the Noon oò
In June 2000, you saw how Assistant Superintendent of Police (ASP), Sunday
Oladipo And Senior Operative of National Drug Law Enforcement Agency
(NDLEA), Ayo Adewunmi were abducted and horse-whipped
By the Oba Morufu:
Guardian Newspaper, Friday June 23, 2000 page13.

Winrin winrin, Priest of the Night oò
In October 2000, you know the causes of O'odua Peoples Congress (OPC)
Factions' clash in Ejigbo - Where, you watched how three persons were killed:
http://allafrica.com/stories/200010130391.html

Awonamajaoò, Ifa Priest of dream-worlds oò
Yepa! Won't you tell us
The causes of the continuation OPC clash in 2001 and 2002 in Ejigbo-
Where many people lost their lives.

Okuku-su-wi, Priest of the mid-night oò
Have you not seen the untold evil in Oba Morufu Ojoola International Market
That people like us do not know?
https://www.facebook.com/sharafa.soladoye/videos/t.1768384232/6949
42410568608/?type=2&theater

Figure 4.3 (Continued)

appear in the court and then were sent into prison immediately. I was in the prison for about five days and I got bail after I've fulfilled the bail condition with others, got released and I faced six solid months rigorous judicial procedure, but at the end of it all, the court thrown out the case.[2]

The arrest would be the first for Atiku. They were charged with "disturbing the peace of the community, intimidating the public, distributing publications likely to provoke the community, and managing an unlawful society" (Front Line Defenders) ("Case History: Jelili Atku"). He was placed in jail for three days. The news of the arrest appeared in many local and international presses:

> On Sunday, award-winning performance artist and human rights activist, Jelili Atiku, was arrested for his performance in the Ejigbo area of Oshodi-Isolo, Lagos state on Thursday the 14th of January, under the instructions of Oba Morufu Ojoola of Ejigbo. While the reason for his arrest was not quite clear then, whether the Oba was offended by the performance itself, or that it was staged without his permission, there was widespread discontent over the unlawful arrest and continued detention of Atiku until his release, on bail, only two days ago.
>
> (Egbedi)

His family was harassed by the police who deployed acts of intimidation by destroying his studio. The legal battle would drag on for six months before the charges were ultimately dropped (Front Line Defenders). The brief time in the prison continues to haunt Atiku,

> I can tell you a part of the experience, because this is away of documenting the experience. When we got into the prison. We got into the cell, we were stripped naked and we're asked to sit down, to stand and they were searching our body. They opened my mouth widely, they were searching if I hide money and they asked me to prostrate by squatting and they spread my anus to see if there's something inside is hiding there. And we're asked to sit down in what they say, 'Cargo yourself,' you'll sit down and somebody sit down very close to you. You'll sit down while your arms is squashed like this, like a squash movement and somebody will sit down very close to you without space.
> And we were like that almost about 30 in a row. It is a kind of a cargo or a cargo movement. And in the night, we slept...

you know the way they shipped slaves during the Atlantic slave trade, that was the way we sleep, head-to-head, shoulder to shoulder no space. And this is how I slept...[3]

He has spoken publicly about the degrading and inhumane condition of the prisons in Nigeria and the ongoing fight for human rights and social justice. The men responsible for the assault and murder that took place at the market in Ejigbo were never found nor arrested.

The Yorùbá faith, an indigenous epistemology, is a form of resistance against necropolitical systems. Atiku's religion provides a critical lens to unravel the multiple political and social structures established by colonization. His embracement and public performance of Yorùbá is an affront to many, particularly politicians, because it openly critiques and generates attention to the continued brutal effects of colonialism in contemporary Nigerian society. There is no post in post-colonialism. For Jelili Atiku, performance is a way of being in the world. Though broadly, his work reminds us to fight against local and global injustices continually. More significantly, he espouses a return to the visceral, to situate and to be present in our bodies. For him, to be in the body is "a revolutionary and spiritual act of resistance."[8]

Notes

1 Myron Beasley interview with Jelili Atiku, July 25, 2020.
2 Myron Beasley interview with Jelili Atiku, July 25, 2020.
3 Myron Beasley interview with Jelili Atiku, July 25, 2020.
4 Myron Beasley interview with Jelili Atiku, July 25, 2020.
5 Myron Beasley interview with Jelili Atiku, July 26, 2020.
6 According to Yorùbá tradition, *Aragamago* was a bird given to Odù, the wife of Ọrúnmìlà, as a sacred power of manifestation, vision, and knowingness to penetrate the past, present, and future. It represents the feminine power of healing.
7 Myron Beasley interview with Jelili, July 26, 2020.
8 Myron Beasley interview with Jelili Atiku, July 25, 2020.

Works Cited

"Case History: Jelili Atku." *Front Line Defenders.* https://www.frontlinedefenders.org/en/case/case-history-jelili-atiku. Accessed May 30 2022.
Drewal, Margaret Thompson. *Yoruba Ritual: Performers, Play, Agency.* Indiana University Press, 1992. vol. Book, Whole.

Editors, museumpublicity.com. *Centre for Contemporary Art, Lagos Presents Jelili Atiku Araferaku.* https://museumpublicity.com/2013/01/21/centre-for-contemporary-art-lagos-presents-jelili-atiku-araferaku/. Accessed May 30 2022.

Egbedi, Hadassah. *Jailed for Art's Sake: On the Unlawful Arrest of Nigerian Artist, Jelili Atiku.* https://venturesafrica.com/jailed-for-arts-sake-on-the-unlawful-arrest-of-nigerian-artist-jelili-atiku/. Accessed May 30 2022.

"Jelili Atiku." www.omenkaoline.com/on-art-politics-and-radicalism/. Accessed June 6 2022.

Mbembe, Achille and Steve Corcoran. *Necropolitics.* Duke University Press, 2019. vol. Book, Whole.

Tewa, Thadde. *Jelili Atiku: Performance Artist & Activist.* https://africanah.org/jelili-atiku-performance-artist-activist/. Accessed May 30 2022.

5 Geographies of Death Wearing White Shoes

We own you.

— A white collector (to Faustine)

New York artist Nona Faustine labors to mark significant places of historical truths of enslaved Africans and African Americans through self-portraiture. By marking the cityscape, Faustine participates in a truth-telling discourse to memorialize the dead and prevent the erasure of a history. The concept of modern democracies, according to Mbembe, is built on mythologies that actively participate in the erasure of history to create a dominant narrative and a fabricated story. Democracies are also built on violence. "The history of modern democracies gets painted as though it reduces to a history internal to Western societies as if closed in on themselves and closed to the immediate environment" (Mbembe 22). Mbembe uses the metaphor of the solar and nocturnal bodies. The solar body extols the beauty of democracy as a perfect society of equality and justice. The nocturnal body which, Mbembe spends more time with is the underbelly, the realities of how the democratic state maintains a perpetual state of colonization and violence. The nocturnal body is the realm in which violence is deployed in a variety of ways, including the absence of the lived realities of marginal communities in the master narrative. "In imagination and in practice, the life of conquered and subjugated natives is represented as a succession of predestined events ... to be legitimated one engages in disavowing and effacing all traces of prior native presence" (Mbembe 25–26). The death and killing of marginal communities are supported through an absence of truth-telling. It is easy to do away with black and brown people if they do not exist in a nation-state's history or grand narrative. The accurate accounts of brutalities toward racial and gendered groups are replaced with a masked universal

DOI: 10.4324/9780429028489-5

reason that portends a narrative of equity, equality, and justice for all (Mbembe 22–23). The premise of the debate surrounding Critical Race Theory in the United States is a struggle for truth-telling or a fabricated reason to maintain a narrative of white supremacy. This chapter considers how visual culture, in this case, the monuments' presence, reflects and influences social policy toward black and brown people. I do so by locating the series, *White Shoes* by photographer Nona Faustine as a memorial to the dead. This chapter situates Faustine's images as a set of performances. To consider the performative framing is to render the images as fluid, encompassing a dynamic range of enactments rather than still visual representations. Therefore, the images are endowed with multiple meanings that crisscross and wrap around the portraits, allowing the viewer to participate in various ways. Interrogating the images as performances also includes the materials used and the actions of the artist making the images. The collection of self-portraitures marks the unmarked spaces of black life that are rendered invisible. Through her black body, she shifts the geography of the cityscape to make known what is in plain sight and unspoken. The series of photographs, which I frame as performances, complicates the concept of a memorial and how to read (see/observe) them and reminds us of the power of visual culture. But first, given the recent fervent protests after the aftermath of the brutal killing of George Floyd, I consider the ongoing debates regarding what are memorials and what should be memorialized. Memorials are sacred shrines for many. "Underneath the terror of the sacred there are missing bones, which are constantly being unearthed," as Mbembe warns (80).

Patience on a Memory

In 2016, I curated the show "Patience on a Memory." The exhibition featured the work of the sculpture Eto Otitigbe. The exhibition was part of the series to attend to the debates at the University of Texas at Austin to address the confederate monuments on the campus. The show acknowledged the complex interplay between public memorializing, history, and everyday life and asked viewers to question how monuments invite audiences to participate in the memory and retelling of significant moments. More importantly, I alerted the audience that: The clad pillars create a performance space between the artists and the unknown audience, soliciting the onlooker to examine, to read, to wonder. The allure of the aesthetic harkens to the excellently crafted artistry of such obelisks. They are mementos of the precious past, or perhaps obstructions to other narratives of that past. Nonetheless, their elegance and regal nature command a passivity, an allegiance to their absoluteness that, when left unattended, seeps into the unconsciousness.

My goal was to inform the audience that monuments "do" things in social spaces that consciously and unconsciously affect us. It also was a moment of thinking about how society remembers and questioning the concept of a monument and what forms a monument can occupy. After a year of comprehensive campus discussions that included public lectures, exhibitions, dance performances, and other forms of debates, the university decided to move several of the confederate monuments (those deemed most offensive) indoors.

More than five years later, while writing this chapter, the world is grappling with the results of systematic oppression caused by colonization. It is two weeks since the horrible murder of George Floyd at the hands of police officers in Minneapolis. As the #*blacklivesmatter* protests invaded the streets nightly from major cities to small rural towns across the United States and worldwide, political actions took a remarkable turn midway through the wave of protests. On Sunday, June 7, 2020, protestors in Bristol, England, toppled an eighteen-foot-tall statue of 17th-century slave trader Edward Colston down from its pedestal and tossed him into the harbor. Some demonstrators re-enacted the chokehold, pressing the knee on the statue's neck, like the police officer that killed Floyd. Edward Colston made his fortune from his company, the Royal African Company (RAC). Colston is responsible for shipping more enslaved individuals to the Americas than any other entity (Siddique and Skopeliti). The very next day, in Richmond, Virginia, protestors hoisted ropes around the eight-foot statue of Christopher Columbus, pulled it down and dragged it 200 feet across the Arthur Ashe Boulevard, and submerged it in the Fountain Lake as the group chanted, "This land is Powhatan land" and "Columbus represents genocide" (Joachim). The same day, across the Atlantic, in Antwerp, the statue of King Leopold, the Belgian King who reigned over the Congo Free State from 1885 to 1908, was removed after protests. Leopold was brutal and responsible for the death of more than 10 million Congolese, half of the population (Pronczuk and Zaveri). The removal of the monuments indicates a seismic shift. I return to the phrase from my statement above, "Nonetheless, their elegance and regal nature command a passivity, an allegiance to their absoluteness that, when left unattended, seeps into the unconsciousness." In the case of the confederate monuments in the United States, most of which were erected after reconstruction to mark exclusionary boundaries and to remind black people of their place in society. The confederate monuments are markers in the landscape of cities directly related to "redlining" and "developing and cleaning" neighborhoods to be refurbished to accommodate whites and the economically privileged to gentrify the communities. The monuments were not only symbolic reminders but physical markers.

Confederate monuments marked literal geographic spaces and cast a shadow that mark non-white bodies through their visual representation. Despite the movement of dismantling colonial and oppressive statues, simultaneously, there is a wave, particularly in the southern United States, of the defacing of historical markers of African Americans (Wagner). In the winter of 2021, bullets riddled the plaque in honor of Mary Turner, who, on May 18, 1918, was thirty-three and eight months pregnant (Georgia Historical Society). She was burned, shot, and mutilated for publicly denouncing the lynching of her husband the day before. The marker is located in rural Hahira, Georgia.

According to Michel-Rolph Trouillot, "Any historical narrative is a bundle of silences." Monuments are unsettling, never representing one monolithic story but rather multiple narratives crisscrossing and wrapping tightly around the memorial, some are hidden and buried underneath. Unless individuals can fully embrace pain, suffering, and death, reminds Maya Lin, they are unable to move forward. Melancholia settles in the uninterrogated memorials, and the haunted ghosts persist prolonging pain, (re) performing trauma. To unearth is to reveal pain, trauma, public secrets, more importantly, it leads and participates in an ongoing dialogue and destabilizes the very thing it seeks to memorialize.

The White Shoes

I went from Lower Manhattan to I think I got as far as Wall Street, the famous picture of me at Wall Street was the slave market. So it's site specific and it's where I'm using my body as a memorial. I'm standing in tribute to those people who actually built the city and urging the city, in a way, to mark these sites.[1]

Trained as a photographer, it was an archeology class that would spark an interest in burial sites of African and African American life in the city of New York. According to Faustine, "The *White Shoes* is about places of slavery in New York where the enslaved lived, died, and are buried or worked."[2] The series is a collection of thirty-seven self-portraits of the artist herself, photographed nude adorned in white shoes marking significant locations throughout New York City. "I started in Brooklyn on the beach," she shares. "The coastline faces the Atlantic and that connection to the slave trade, the Trans-Atlantic slave trade. But also, they used to smuggle slave ships up the coast of what was then called Long Island. Even after the New York embargoed slavery."[3] The image taken at that site is titled *Like a Pregnant Corpse the Ship Expelled Her into the Patriarchy.* Faustine rests on her back, nude, atop the black rocks of the Long Island shoreline wearing the white pumps. Another at the same site, titled, *Even the Comfort of a Stone Would be a Gain.*

The artist on her side, with her hands pillowing her head as if sleeping. So striking, vulnerable, audacious, I paused the first time I witnessed Faustine's images. She plans, arranges, and sets up the camera, only needing an assistant to press the button. Faustine's process of making the images, particularly in this context, the use of her body, opens an array of critical questions, including what it means for her to turn the gaze on the black female body. McKittrick aptly articulates how the black female body is configured in social geographic space:

> Geographically, the category of "black woman" evidenced human/inhuman and masculine/feminine racial organization. The classification of black femininity as therefore also a process of placing her within the broader system of servitude — as an inhuman racial-sexual worker, as an objectified body, as a site through which sex, violence, and reproduction can be imagined and enacted, and as a captive human. Her classificatory racial-sexual body, then, determined her whereabouts in relation to her humanity.
>
> (xvii)

And what does it mean when Faustine anchors her body in a specific place? She encourages a rethinking, or should I say a re-looking. "Unlike memorial plagues, Faustine's images require an effort on the viewer's part, who now needs to retain her eye to follow different patterns of spatial organization" (Grujić). The sites highlighted by Faustine are not explicitly hidden but, in most cases, unmarked. The *White Shoes* is a memorial to significant unmarked spaces as to memorialize and help us remember a black history and thus participates in a rupture in the discourse of the nocturnal body (In the language of Mbembe), the true history and realities that are obscured by the democratic state. Also, as Faustine locates her body, her nude black voluptuous body, the focus of the images challenges the visual codes of the female body in mainstream Eurocentric visual culture and affirms black femaleness. For example, take the two images mentioned above, *Like a Pregnant Corpse the Ship Expelled Her into the Patriarchy* and *Even the Comfort of a Stone Would be a Gain*; Faustine's body is a memorial to the black female enslaved. In reading the images, not lost are those who arrived at that shore, many who died, those who survived were birthed to uphold white patriarchy. The title of the images allows for speculative possibilities. Other sites include the Dutch Pre-Revolutionary cemetery in Brooklyn, where three slaves are buried among the colonists. In my interview with Faustine, she reflects:

> Three enslaved people buried in it who were deemed special enough to be buried with the people who own them. And that's a pre-revolutionary site and it's very loaded with some of the wealthiest New Yorkers who owned slaves. A lot of those families got their fortune from slave trading.

The Tweed Courthouse at fifty-two Chambers Street and the Supreme Court at twenty Centre Street are other locations that Faustine highlights. At the New York Supreme Court, the artist, stands strikingly close to the ornate Corinthian column. A profile shot presents her powerful stance as she gazes forward with her hands to her side. The title of this image is *Judgement Day, 60 Supreme Court, New York City*. Another from the same site, *Over my dead body*, pictures Faustine walking up the grand granite steps, naked, holding old rusted shackles in her left hand. The performances overtly signal that the sites are built on African and African American burial grounds. The buildings themselves were constructed by the enslaved, and a stark reminder that by 1775, New York City harbored more enslaved people than any other colony except Charleston, South Carlina (Harrington). A historical truth that is often erased from the history books. Faustine recalls: "It is an awakening for Black New Yorkers because before that we were all taught in that New York City didn't have much slavery; we didn't have Black people here, we freed the slaves fairly early we're not a slave state."[4] She continues, with an astonishing statement of fact: "One thing about the colonists: they kept really good records. Dutch, British, all of them. There were censuses of enslavers and how many slaves they kept, even sometimes their names. They are all there in the archives."[5] The documents bearing truth exist but are avoided in the grand narrative (Figure 5.1).

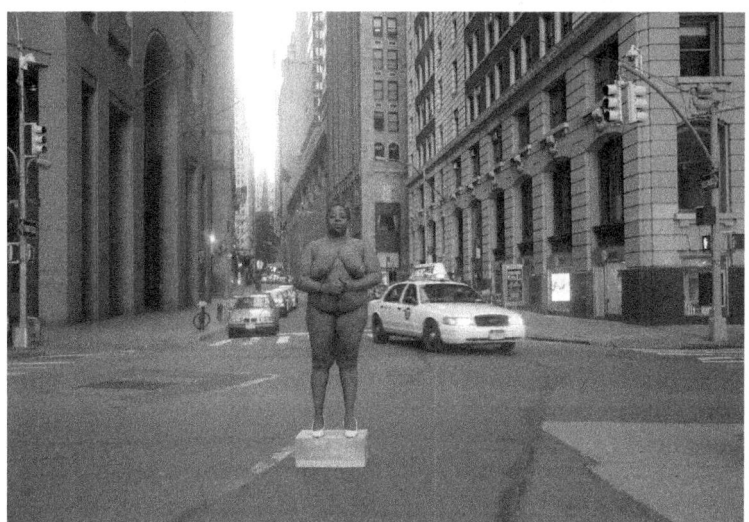

Figure 5.1 From Her Body Came Their Greatest Wealth. Courtesy of Nona
Faustine.

The image made on Wall Street between Water and Pearl streets
highlights the site of a slave market. In the image titled *From Her
Body Came Their Greatest Wealth* (Figure 5.1), Faustine stands atop
a wooden box in the middle of the intersection of the Financial Dis-
trict. Wearing but her white shoes, her hands clasp under her stom-
ach, breasts exposed, she stares forward. As cars crisscross around
her, she shoots during a 38-degree morning rush hour in March;
Faustine claims:

> I put the block in front on that site, where the slave market
> was, and I just started photographing and it took 30 minutes.
> At different points, the traffic was flowing down Wall Street,
> then it would stop and then come down Water Street, and the
> cars would just keep going around me, completely naked. They
> didn't care. No one said a thing… No one said a thing. No horn
> was blown. No one stopped—the whole 30 minutes.[6]

A slave market, Wall Street's first commodity was selling humans,
black humans, which is another historical truth that is not too readily known and absent from textbooks. Even as Faustine makes the
images, in the morning at the bustling intersection, her black naked
female body remains invisible as drivers and passersby's go about

their morning as if she is not standing in the carrefour completely naked.

Another site of performance is in the Bronx, amid the warehouses in the Hunts Point area is the location of Joseph Rodman Drake Park. In the park's center are old gravestones, which are portioned off by a gate. The graves of prominent Bronx families such as Willett, Leggett, Tiffany, and Hunt are within the gated area. In 2013, a group of elementary school students discovered the site of more than forty-four graves of African and Native Americans enslaved just opposite the fence. In the image, *What the Mind Forgets the Soul Remembers*, Faustine wears a white summer dress, white stocking, and white pumps, her face obscured with an African mask as she sits outside the gated cemetery under a willow tree. The African mask is an overt performance of surrogation, her body not only stands in for the dead, but Faustine evokes a transatlantic diasporic ritual performance. Like the Women of the Good Death, who promenade through the streets of Cacheria in the same attire seen here, Faustian harkens ceremonial enactments to honor the dead.

The *White Shoe* performances attend to the cultural politics of memorializing and truth-telling. Through her black female body, Faustine asks us to look anew at the landscape and typographies to relearn the city and thus reveal the true narratives and the persistent ghosts of trauma, pain, genocide that continue to haunt us.

In many ways, Faustine is reminding us that modernity is haunted by its histories of war, murder, death, and genocide. Yet it is the ever presence of amnesia that encourages a looking away. The sisterhood of the Good Death, to which I referred earlier in this book, walk through the streets of Cacheria not only to affirm their presence but to acknowledge and honor the deaths that took place on the streets of the city. The concept of memorializing in the context of many Africana cosmologies is an ongoing engagement with the dead. To memorialize is not to simply erect a shrine to the dead; it is a daily engagement with the ancestorial spirits for guidance (Beasley "Curatorial Studies on the Edge: The Ghetto Biennale, a Junkyard, and the Performance of Possibility"). To tend to the haunts is to close the gap between the atrocities of modernity and amnesia. African Americans consciously or unconsciously engage in a persistent haunting and madness associated with the transatlantic slave trade and colonialism that positions black bodies as landless. The land of the New World was built and cultivated by the enslaved but never owned by them. The *White Shoe* project asks what it means to have a connection to land for a person of African descent after being relegated and placed in localities. McKittrick, a black feminist human geographer, claims black bodies occupy a perpetual state of landlessness because they are placed in New World grids that are "economically, racially, and sexually normative, or, seemingly nonblack" and that "suppresses the possibility of black geographies by invalidating the subject's cartographic needs, expressions, and knowledges" (McKittrick 2–3). In the United States, organizations such as the National Community Reinvestment Coalition (NCRC) are consistent with compiling and disseminating research that details the ongoing effects of redlining. The most recent study, compiled by the NCRC, regarding why people of color are disproportionately contracting COVID-19 and why they are more likely to have underlying health conditions are significant. The study indicates many people of color are more likely to live or have grown up in neighborhoods that expose them to damaging health threats such as poor housing quality and environmental pollutants (Harris, Prener). For example, in 2022, in Lowndes County, Alabama, where the population is three-quarters African American, most live with little access to and infrastructure for clean water and no septic sanitation systems (Okeowo).

It is misleading to deny the power of geography and its effects on identity, personhood, and belonging. The New World grids are spaces where people of color have been forced to live (i.e., redlining, transatlantic slave trade) and a discursive formation that prevents economic expansion, educational advancement, and quality healthcare. Faustine's work is significant because it ruptures the discourse of the master narrative but specifically interrogates the cityscape and how a grid of a city can function as a tool of white supremacist patriarchy. Du Bois' *The Philadelphia Negro* did not only map the details of the African American community revealing the diversity that exists but also the exclusionary politics that allowed for crime, poverty, and illiteracy to suggest the (New World) grids are bound by a racial ideology that profoundly influences everyday lived experiences. McKittrick's use of the slave ship as a metaphor for the instability of geography is fitting. The ship, she suggests, functions to conceal and dehumanize, but "importantly, black subjectivity is not swallowed up by the ship itself. Rather, the ship, its crew, black subjects, the ocean, and ports make geography what it is, a location through which a moving technology can create differential and contextual histories" (McKittrick xii). The ship then is not only an object of concealment, but a lens through which, people of African descent articulate pain and horror thus giving new meaning of the ship. Faustine, through the explicit use of her body, reminds us of the links between the practices of domination and black female bodies with forced locations and racial and sexual violence. McKittrick writes about the conundrum between space, representation, and the black female body:

> Race becomes attached to place in detrimental ways because local conditions reify and naturalize identity-difference: black women live in "bad"/black neighborhoods, have unhealthy children, restricted employment opportunities and resources, longer workdays, and so on. Or: polluted + inexpensive regions = unhealthy/black dwellings = subhuman/sub-woman/ bad mother.
>
> (13)

Black geographies are alternative patterns on the grids, carved out spaces of cultural production and affirmation. Faustine's contemporary, 20th-century body is looking back to negotiate and critically unravel the oppressive systems of today to hopefully begin the process of liberation, affirmation, and inclusive politics. By marking the spaces with her black female body, she complicates the line between body eroticism and exclusion. The use of her nude body, Faustine, unapologetically demands that you look at her. The looking is an interrogation of the self and all the discourses surrounding her body. She is black. She is big. She is naked and thus fully exposed and vulnerable. She stands with all the weight of the world on those white shoes. To look at her is to critique self and society.

Faustine is a connection between the past and present and thus, through the use of her black body, expands localities with time and space. The *White Shoes* is a summons to endeavor the lingering trauma and discomfort that is obscured, as Mbembe reminds us, by constant amnesia that keeps us looking away as to deny people, histories, and truth. Faustine's images as a public performance are an un-telling of the master narrative and allow for speculative possibilities, insisting that the sites themselves are not static but part of a dialectic performance. The *White Shoe* performances connect the present with the past with memory, history, knowledge and help us rethink black geographies that could help us reveal spatial discourses of death.

Coda

While writing this chapter in New Orleans and attending proceedings of the Prospect #5 Triennial, a personal highlight was witnessing the unveiling of the sculpture *Sentinel (Mami Wata)* (2020–21) by Simone Leigh. The sculpture is placed in front of the enormous columns of which the Confederate Robert E. Lee statue once stood. The *Sentinel (Mami Wata)* sculpture was not placed on the empty column but instead in front of it. An art critic was disappointed that the Leigh sculpture was not placed on top and a direct replacement of the confederate statue. I celebrated the placement of the *Sentinel (Mami Wata)* in front of the column to make the art piece accessible (instead of looking up) but how it encourages a different way of participating in looking and thinking about monuments. To have placed the *Sentinel (Mami Wata)* on top would suggest a stand in for Robert E. Lee and recall the confederate history. Instead, by placing the sculpture in front, Leigh disrupts what stood there before and insists on a different narrative anew.

Notes

1 Interview with Myron Beasley, May 21, 2021.
2 Interview with Myron Beasley, May 21, 2021.
3 Brooklyn used to be called Long Island. In the images, Faustine is in Brooklyn, Coney Island, the coast of which faces the Atlantic.
4 Interview with Myron Beasley, May 21, 2021.
5 Interview with Myron Beasley, May 21, 2021.
6 Interview with Myron Beasley, May 21, 2021.

Works Cited

Beasley, Myron M. "Curatorial Studies on the Edge: The Ghetto Biennale, a Junkyard, and the Performance of Possibility." *Journal of Curatorial Studies*, vol. 1, no. 17. 2012, pp. 65–81.

Du Bois, W. E. B. *The Philadelphia Negro,* vol. no. 14., Kraus-Thomson Organization Ltd, 1973. vol. Book, Whole.

Grujić, Ana. "Black Geographies of Struggle and Pleasure in Nona Faustine's White Shoes." *Women & Performance*, vol. 29, no. 2, 2019, pp. 146–61, https://go.exlibris.link/d0L6dPmB.

Harrington, Spencer P. M. "Bones & Bureaucrats." *Archaeology*, vol. 46, no. 2, 1993, pp. 28–38.

Harris, Rita T. "Environmental Justice and Covid-19: Some Are Living in a Syndemic." *National Community Reinvestment Coalition* https://ncrc.org/environmental-justice-and-covid-19-some-are-living-in-a-syndemic/. Accessed April 21 2022.

Joachim, Zach. "Columbus Statue Removed from Lake Wednesday after It Was Torn Down at Byrd Park." *Richmond Local News* https://richmond. com/news/local/columbus-statue-removed-from-lake-wednesday-after-it-was-torn-down-at-byrd-park-late/article_8a009c9c-1c5d-5e2a-a3bf-0b015a8a2277.html. Accessed August 22 2022.

Mary Turner and the Lynching Rampage of 1918. Georgia Historical Society https://georgiahistory.com/ghmi_marker_updated/mary-turner-and-the-lynching-rampage-of-1918/. Accessed August 22 2022.

Mbembe, Achille and Steve Corcoran. *Necropolitics.* Duke University Press, 2019. vol. Book, Whole.

McKittrick, Katherine. *Demonic Grounds: Black Women and the Cartographies of Struggle.* N - New ed., University of Minnesota Press, 2006. vol. Book, Whole.

Okeowo, Alexis. "The Heavy Toll of the Black Belt's Wastewater Crisis." *The New Yorker* https://www.newyorker.com/magazine/2020/11/30/the-heavy-toll-of-the-black-belts-wastewater-crisis. Accessed April 21 2022.

Prener, Christopher G. "Demographic Change, Segregation, and the Emergence of Peripheral Spaces in St. Louis, Missouri." *Elsevier,* vol. 133, 2021, 102472. https://www.sciencedirect.com/science/article/pii/S0143622821000886.

Pronczuk, Monika and Mihir Zaveri. "Statue of Leopold Ii, Belgian King Who Brutalized Congo, Is Removed in Antwerp." *New York Times* https://www.nytimes.com/2020/06/09/world/europe/king-leopold-statue-antwerp.html. Accessed August 22 2022.

"Redlining and Neighborhood Health." *National Community Reinvestment Coalition* https://ncrc.org/holc-health/.

Siddique, Haroon and Clea Skopeliti. "Blm Protesters Topple Statue of Bristol Slave Trader Edward Colston." *The Guardian* https://www. theguardian.com/uk-news/2020/jun/07/blm-protesters-topple-statue-of-bristol-slave-trader-edward-colston. Accessed August 22 2022.

Trouillot, Michel-Rolph and Hazel V. Carby. *Silencing the Past: Power and the Production of History.* Beacon Press, 2015. vol. Book, Whole.

Wagner, James. "A Marker Honoring Jackie Robinson Was Defaced. M.L.B. Helped Replace It." *New York Times* https://www.nytimes. com/2022/01/27/sports/baseball/jackie-robinson-mlb-georgia.html? referringSource=articleShare. Accessed August 22 2022.

6   On Rituals of Death

While dismissing the reasons behigen entification and leaving little room for the public to ask "why this enemy now?" the necropolitical sovereign decides on the order of life and death based on which it then proceeds to perform a legalized ritual of death—be it in the form of a national criminal justice system or a project of genocide and ethnic cleansing in near and far war theaters. This performance is scripted, Mbembe has it, in line with a primal binary that distinguishes between "those who must live and those who must die"
—Mahshid Mayar, *Feasts of Indifference: Racialization, Affect, and Necropolitics*

Mayar's comment is revealing as to how the sovereign state can have the capacity to use the concept of ritual performance as a tool to justify genocide. "Ritual performances come naturally and flows organically," claims Nathalie Anguezomo Mba Bikoro, "it is a means by which I lead the community into challenging socially oppressive systems."[1] After witnessing one of her performances in 2015 and following her career since Bikoro is consumed with putting to death colonial legacies. She wishes to bury monuments and statues of colonialism and create theaters, cultural spaces, and libraries in their stead. She seeks to achieve this task through ritual performance. Born in Gabon and educated in England and France, Bikoro is currently based in Berlin. Her work is situated steep in ritual performance and advances theoretical dialogues about decolonization and indigeneity in the global South. Bikoro, who identifies as a queer African woman, comes from a family of political activists. She is the granddaughter of Léon M'ba, the first President of Gabon (post-independence). Her family continued to face persecution long after his death in 1967. Diagnosed with leukemia at the age of five, while undergoing experimental treatments

DOI: 10.4324/9780429028489-6

in the Netherlands, she recalls the nurses encouraging her to "force the pain out through creative actions." As an adult she seeks to eliminate the pain of continued hostility toward Indigenous and native people through creative actions for which she foregrounds themes of trauma, archive, narrative, and identity.

Bikoro's work is concerned with transnational and intercultural dialogues regarding the oppressive legacies of colonialism primarily of the southern hemisphere. Earlier in this text, I refer to Gilroy's concept of *The Black Atlantic* which foregrounds the flow from England to the Americas and the Caribbean. Specifically, it creates reciprocal creative exchanges across the Atlantic. Bikoro's work is significant because it allows us to think about the complex web of interaction between Indigenous communities of the global South. Furthermore, to think about performance and the flows of creative transactions in Joseph Roach's concept of circum-Atlantic, which "insists on the centrality of the diasporic and genocidal histories of African and the American, North and South in the creation of the culture of modernity" (Roach). Roach contemplates Dryden's *The Indian Emperor* as staged symbolic representations of intercultural encounters or, should I say, colonial encounters in which blacks, natives, and whites interacted. The key phrase is "staged symbolic representations" that create fictional narratives reproduced as fact in the historical retelling and simultaneously functioned as a form of erasure. In the account of the fictional narrative, the accurate histories of violence and the genocide is obscured. Nevertheless, the circum-Atlantic performance allows for ways to contemplate transactional knowledge, creative energies, and a sense of being among native and Indigenous African and Latin American communities. The use of ritual in community is significant but Somé alerts the sacred and communal action is also a critique to Western societies:

> The problem with Western culture is that it is a show-off culture that intimidates. This is why it is generating so much death, loss and displacement. To perform ritual for show is to generate some kind of death or loss. Concealment of ritual is an act of life preservation because it is only in its concealment that needs are met that cannot be met in any other way.
>
> (Somé)

The centrality of ritual performance in everyday life is a link shared between communities of the global South and one of which Bikoro makes use.

In this segment, I foreground two performances of the *Sun Dance* anthology and I consider, Bikoro's performances as theory. "Ritual is, above all else, the yardstick by which people measure their state of connection with the hidden ancestral realm," opines Africana theorist Somé (Somé). For many Indigenous cultures, ritual performance is a way to connect and tap into the ancestral world for guidance. Somé uses the term "modern world" to describe "non-Indigenous" forms of knowledge. The "modern world" pulls individuals away from the central force of the ancestral world and nature and thus produces alienation from the self and the destruction of the community. Bikoro proclaims, "I do not consider this work to be art—or performance ... it is ritual, and it is process."[2] Her statement reveals her insistence that knowledge production and theory-making are in the doing, the actual performing of the rituals she leads. Her performance is theory. The argument is also a critique of Western academia, where performance and theater studies locate its history on rituals from native and Indigenous cultures. Western academia foregrounds the aesthetic and kinesthetic and honors the "symbolic" gestures for transitions and ceremony, but epistemological or spiritual dimensions are disregarded. The criticism is also lodged against the primacy of a European standard of beauty and the artificial divide between fine arts and craft. Through ritual performance, Bikoro both summons and acknowledges other forms of knowledge production she labels as "epistemologies to address narrative, archive, and trauma" and bring attention to the brutal lived realities of black and Indigenous women.[3]

Bikoro's performances are lengthy, durational, evoking visceral ritual practices, with some lasting an hour to several days to a couple of months and even multi-yearlong segments. *After Sundance, On Indigenous Resistance* is an anthology of performances commencing in 2013 and concluding in 2018. The title *Sundance* is derived from Sun Dance, a distinctly sacred ceremony of many Indigenous communities in the Americas.[4]

Bikoro's *After Sundance* comprises six embodied performances in Brazil, Columbia, Mexico, and Canada. Each performance is unique, often held on sacred Indigenous sites, and is collaborative. For example, *All of Our Mothers (Future Monuments),* performed with Kainai First Nation interdisciplinary artist Terrance Houle, is a visually interactive experience and an experimental sense-memory project that examine the role of memory and colonial histories. The action, taking place in Fort Calgary, Canada, concludes with developing a time machine of eleven opera scores derived from narratives of migration. Moreover, in *How many stones can be free* (2013), an act that responds to the tribal disputes and violence in Bikoro's home country, Gabon, and globally, where violence occurs more than speaking and creating a dialogue. Mutual dialogic exchange is often muted because of cultural and systemic historical legacies that have rendered communities silent. She insists the audience play a game of breaking glass bottles; Bikoro skips along the broken charred bits of glass, leaving behind a trail of blood— the path of muted and silent voices. I highlight two performative actions, *The Burial* and *El Carrusel or Au Hazard Balthazar* as they exemplify the scope and breadth of her creative, intellectual, and political engagements and, more significantly, highlight the treatment of native and Indigenous women in the global South.

Femicide is a term that means the intentional killing of girls and women because they are female. The term is often used to highlight the oppression and violence against women. Discussions regarding the killing of native and Indigenous women in the Americas continues to be overlooked by the media and government systems. In 2014, Indigenous women were murdered at six times the rate of non-Indigenous women in Canada (Klingspohn; Smiley). The Royal Canadian Mounted Police have recorded 1,181 cases of murdered and/or disappeared Indigenous women and girls over a thirty-year period (Klingspohn; Smiley). In Colombia, from 2000 to 2004, one woman died every day, and one woman disappeared every fifteen days for political reasons (Tovar-Restrepo and Irazábal). In 2009, 70% of human rights violations against Indigenous individuals between 1998 and 2009 were against women and children (Joseph). Joseph has titled this crisis in the United States as "A Modern Trail of Tears." Drawing from data from the National Missing and Unidentified Persons System (NamUs), the National Crime Information Center (NCIC), and from data collected and published in a report produced by the Urban Indian Health Institute (UIHI), all suggest homicide is the third leading cause of death among women and girls between ten and twenty-four years of age, and the fifth leading cause of death among women between twenty-five and thirty-four years of age among Native American and Alaskan natives. Most of the organizations mentioned above provide a disclaimer that no formal mechanism exists to document missing and violence against native women, therefore the numbers are higher than what is reported. More significantly, Joseph argues the crisis of missing and murdered Indigenous women (MMIW) is but one symptom of a greater crisis of violence and oppression affecting Indigenous people today but rather systematic actions beginning with colonization that contribute to the precarious nature of Indigenous and native women.

In 2010 Bikoro, after spending several years in the Norogachi region of Chihuahua, Mexico studying the history of native communities and the disappearance of several friends from the Rarámuri community, her interest in the femicide of native women intensified. The performance *Burial* is a response to horrific history of colonialism, forced labor practices in the mines and mills, and the current realties of violence against native women. According to Bikoro, by the 18th century the native population in Mexico had been reduced to less than 10% of the population (Figure 6.1).

The performance takes place on a mountain where native women are routinely raped and stoned and left to die. It is common to have the rapes videotaped and sold online. Bikoro walks to the site holding a pan of gold paint in which she dips her feet after several steps, thus creating a trail of gold footprints to the burial ground. She disrobes and lays her naked body on the bare earth at the site. Community members were asked to place stones on her body until completely covered. She remained buried for six hours. The performance is a ritual to mourn the loss of native women. The concept of burial is significant because some communities will not bury the

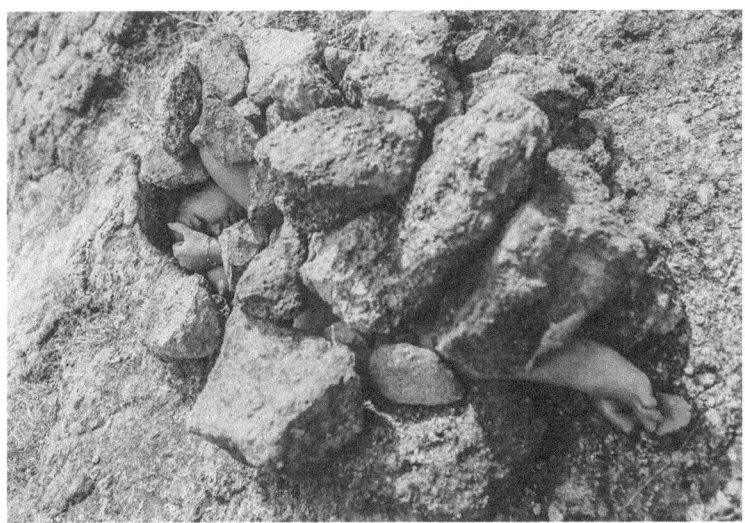

Figure 6.1 The Burial. Photographs by Luis Luján, Leonardo Martínez, Graciela Ovejero Postigo, and Tomas Ruller.

found bodies believing they have been contaminated and therefore cannot undergo spiritual rites of the community. Bikoro contends that her performances are to lead the community to a space of contemplation. For her, the experience is energetic as she reflects on the six hours she was entombed as a "spiritual" journey that includes visits and conversations with native women who had disappeared from that vary site. Bikoro emerges as an interlocutor between the spiritual and physical realms. In addition to this performance, she held meditation workshops on voice and ancestral healing with native women. Her work as an artist is to mobilize and advance social policy against femicide.

El Carusel or Au Hazard Balthazar is a site-specific project that commemorates the lives of and contemporary politics toward native communities in Bogota. More broadly, the project gives prominence to the profound lingering destructive ghosts of colonialism. The performance is inspired by the noted film *Au Hasard Balthazar.* The 1966 film directed by Bresson is an adaptation of Dostoevsky's novel, *The Idiot.* The film follows the treatment of a donkey and its relationship with a family. The donkey represents humankind. Bikoro also admits the influence of *The Girl who fell from the sky.* A memoir that chronicles the life of a young woman dealing with loss, trauma, and truth (Durrow). The site is the *Parque del Independencia*, a former amusement park, but also a site of tourism and a sacred energy point of ritual engagement among some native communities in Columbia.

Bikoro activates an old carousel at the park by leading a donkey around the old machine. Bananas, representing the lynching of native bodies, are placed in a wire extending from the cover of the carousel. At each turn around the bananas are lowered as the crowd joins in to help push the old rotating machine as Le Grand Kallé (aka Joseph Kabasele), *Independence Cha Cha*, plays in the background, but as the day progresses into the evening, the sound slowly morphs into the howling sound of women. The seemingly facile performance is complex in the transcultural and transnational meshing. Bikoro draws on shared histories, creative production, and politics to articulate the similarities of the transatlantic communities and to build solidary against genocidal politics.

The use of the old carousal signals a history of amusement and entertainment that once occurred on that site, and childhood-like vulnerability and naivety cannot be dismissed. The colonial settlers, in some instances, were met with good faith efforts and trust by the Indigenous communities. Still, colonials were about the domination of land to gain natural resources (gold, silver, etc.). The violence also included the introduction of diseases that obliterated entire native and Indigenous communities and cultures. Bikoro's use of the donkey, is thought-provoking. An animal "known" as the universal symbol of stubbornness and a metaphor for mankind, the donkey is a spiritual animal in some native cultures. A highly intelligent and wise animal who has the capacity to ease burdens. Donkeys assist and support when the load is unbearable.

The song *Independence Cha Cha* was inspired by the famous Congolese singer and activist Kallé's participation in "The Round Table Conference." The gathering took place in 1960 to negotiate the Congolese independence from both France and Belgium. The song not only voices the meaning of independence from colonization and demands that it happen immediately but also proposes that the fight for independence is ongoing and a process. *Independence Cha Cha* is the quintessential example of Kallé's style mixing traditional Congolese beats with Cuban rhythms. The use of transatlantic cultural production to evoke the meaning of two countries that are sites of political activism against colonialism is masterful. As the evening progresses Kallé's rhythmic notes morph into a symphony of piercing screams and shrilling howls as the sun sets. And those who participated and witnessed the event were left with the haunting reminder of the persistent violence and killing of Indigenous and native women globally. The necropolitical sovereign, according to Mbembe, through scripted performances sanctions rituals of death (genocide and ethnic cleansing), through national policies, wars, and national criminal justice systems. Bikoro's use of ritual recalls humanity and leads individuals toward contemplation and morality drawn from Indigenous epistemologies. The power of Bikoro's ritual performances is that they force us to examine past atrocities to realize the past is present.

Notes

1 Interview with Myron Beasley on June 30, 2020.
2 Interview with Myron Beasley, June 30, 2020.
3 Interview with Myron Beasley, June 30, 2020.
4 The Sun Dance is the most sacred of rituals of native communities in the Americas, particularly those in the plain state regions and Canada. Communities are to pray for healing as individuals make personal sacrifices for the sake of the community as whole. In 1883, the ritual was criminalized in the US and Canada, but native communities continued the practice in secrecy. The ban was lifted in 1951 (Canada) and 1978 (US). Non-natives are not allowed to participate nor are cameras and video recordings permitted.

Works Cited

Durrow, Heidi W. *The Girl Who Fell from the Sky.* First ed., Algonquin Books of Chapel Hill, 2010. vol. Book, Whole.

Joseph, A. Skylar. "A Modern Trail of Tears: The Missing and Murdered Indigenous Women (Mmiw) Crisis in the Us." *Journal of Forensic and Legal Medicine,* vol. 79, 2021, 102136 https://go.exlibris.link/mvy1WnjC.

Klingspohn, Donna M. "The Importance of Culture in Addressing Domestic Violence for First Nation's Women." *Frontiers in Psychology,* vol. 9, 2018, pp. 872–72, https://go.exlibris.link/MF8d0cqt.

Mayar, Mahshid. "Feasts of Indifference: Racialization, Affect, and Necropolitics in 1x War Games." *European Journal of American Studies,* vol. 16, no. 3, 2021, https://go.exlibris.link/q29TG6kF.

Roach, Joseph. *Cities of the Dead: Circum-Atlantic Performance.* Columbia University Press, 2021. vol. Book, Whole.

Smiley, Cherry. "A Long Road Behind Us, a Long Road Ahead: Towards an Indigenous Feminist National Inquiry." *Canadian Journal of Women and the Law,* vol. 28, no. 2, 2016, pp. 308–13, https://go.exlibris.link/Pk9dldgz.

Somé, Malidoma Patrice. *Ritual: Power, Healing and Community.* Swan/Raven, 1993. vol. Book, Whole.

———. *Ritual: Power, Healing and Community.* Penguin, 1997, p. 39.

Tovar-Restrepo, Marcela and Clara Irazábal. "Indigenous Women and Violence in Colombia: Agency, Autonomy, and Territoriality." *Latin American Perspectives,* vol. 41, no. 1, 2014, pp. 39–58, JSTOR, http://www.jstor.org/stable/24573975.

7 Harlem/Waste, Death, and Newly Assigned Value

> I have a love for Harlem, but more than my love for Harlem, I have a love for black people. I have a love for people that look like me, that move like me, that is everything that I think that is rich in culture. And because I have such a love for black people throughout the diaspora, I feel my duty as an artist to represent that love of black people, or to represent black people to the best of my ability.
> Dianne Smith

In 2012, Dianne Smith, the Harlem-based artist, embarked on a project about trash. The thought emerged when she noticed how much trash she collected in her New York apartment. When Smith matriculated into graduate school, she decided the topic of trash would be the focus of her thesis. Little did she know then how the interrogation of trash would lead her to contemplate the connections between race and gentrification. The abstract artist would identify as a multidisciplinary artist as she encumbered different tools and engaged in various media to address the themes of race, consumption, and gentrification. Smith is an archivist fascinated with objects and how they transmit and retain cultural and historical significance. As indicated in the above quote, Smith is dedicated to the neighborhood of Harlem. Through her concept of "newly assigned value," she examines material culture far beyond the object itself to make pronouncements on cultural and political issues in her neighborhood. In this chapter, I discuss Dianne Smith's use of paper and archival visual images to address gentrification which she reads as the death of black culture, domestic abuse, and the construction of affirming black identities. Specifically, I provide a brief history of Harlem to outline the political systems set in place to allow for the current wave of "redevelopment" responsible

DOI: 10.4324/9780429028489-7

for the rapidly deceasing black populations; I then consider three installations: "Between Harlem and Me," "Uptown Parade," and "STUFF" by Dianne Smith as an attempt to preserve the history of black life in Harlem and gentrification.

Born in South Bronx to two Belizean parents and spending a portion of her childhood living between Belize and New York City, Smith has learned to negotiate living between cultures. As a young adult she left New York and lived for many years in Europe and Los Angeles, when she decided to become a full-time artist, returned to New York and for more than thirty years she has called the Harlem neighborhood home. Smith shares why she choose Harlem as a place to practice her art:

> It wasn't until my twenties that I learned fully of the Harlem Renaissance. And I was Dumbfounded by that, because I went to a school in Harlem for the arts, and never once did anyone take me to the Studio Museum. And so, when I learned about the history and culture from that very artistic perspective, and I decided I wanted to be a maker, there was no other place I wanted to live or be, than Harlem. So, I made a conscious decision to move back to New York, to be an artist and live in Harlem. And maybe it was a little naïve and idealistic because I was thinking, oh, I'm going to be like Zora Neale Hurston and Langston Hughes, and Lois Mailou Jones. I was going to be like all those people and come to Harlem and be this creative person. And in a way, I'm glad I was so naive about that, because it landed me in a place, and I was able to experience Harlem from all its cultural, and all the isms that it was when I moved here, very openly and very organically.[1]

Her daily walks through the city piqued her interest in waste and consumption. In her August book *Waste and Want*, cultural historian Susan Strasser claims that the nature of trash has changed in the 20th century. Insisting that the concept of waste within the Western Hemisphere that once was associated with worn-out, broken and beyond repair objects is now defined as a replacement for out-of-date things (the rapid change of the nature of objects due to technology) for something new and the discarding of things for the sake of space. Strasser, unlike Michael Thompson and his articulation of rubbish theory, connects the concepts of waste with marginality. We tend to place our waste away from the center of our daily livelihood—in the far reaches of the backyard, in the basement, and even in the outskirts of the city in specific neighborhoods. Waste tends to be placed in areas where populations are considered abject and dirty.

Smith's thesis research traces the link between waste, communities like Harlem, and race. Smith recalls a conversation she had with a friend who was born in Honduras and who, like Smith, grew up in the New York area, reflecting on the perceptions of consumption and waste from their international home countries:

> We talked about picking mangoes, plantains, and coconuts off the trees in the yard. We talked about how sacks once used for flour, coffee, or sugar were transformed into clothing and passed down to the younger members of the family or other kids in the community. We shared our memories of dresser drawers being used as a type of bassinet for premature babies, old teapots becoming planters in the yard, dried coconut leaves woven together to create mattresses for the beds, how dried gourds became water scoopers. ...Walls were neatly decorated with old newspapers and magazines, creating beautiful mosaics of images and colors. Art of all kinds was made with whatever was available. In other words, almost everything had a newly assigned value.[2]

But in Harlem, Smith observed how the relationship between discarded items was viewed differently. After weeks of critically exploring her consumption and that of her neighbors and interviewing community members about the growing number of changes in the neighborhood. Like the Starbucks and the Whole Foods at the corner of 125th and Lenox and the sudden appearance of the Church of Latter-Day Saints church at 128th and Lenox. The development signaled an increase in the cost of living and demographic movement in the community. Through her profound study of trash, Smith marked the changing shifts of the Harlem community to reveal the wily politics of gentrification, and how such "redevelopment of communities participates in the displacement of people, and the annihilation of culture." She pondered the question, what does it mean when politicians say they want to "clean the city?" (Smith). Smith as an archivist, is rethinking everyday objects to address social issues and to affirm black identity.

Harlem

> I can tell you that no matter where I go in the world, when I get
> back to Harlem, I know I'm home. There's a sense of belonging,
> and family, that exists in Harlem for me as a black woman, that
> I have not felt any place else.[3]

Smith shares her love for the neighborhood like many other Black
Americans. Situated north of Central Park, Harlem was developed
in the late 18th century by the Dutch as a suburb. By 1811, as part of
a redevelopment plan for Manhattan, the farmland and rural residential domiciles were placed on a grid similar to lower Manhattan
to encourage development because of population growth. By 1904
with the advancement of the subway system, there was an antic-
ipated population surge in the neighborhood. Luxurious hotels
and Brownstones were constructed quickly, but the abundant real
estate exceeded the demand, and many newly formed spaces were
uninhabited and because the then Harlem's middle class moved
out to the outer boroughs, it led to an oversupply of housing stock.
House owners were unable to find renters among the white resi-
dents; therefore, they opened their stock to the black community.
A timely gesture given by 1910, the "great migration" of African
Americans from the South was sojourning northward and began to
occupy the empty, readily available housing. Other migratory flows
followed, such as from the Caribbean in the 1920s and the influx of
Puerto Ricans in the 1950s.

Harlem became recognized as a black Mecca, a beacon of
black intellectualism, artistic expression, and political activism.
From the Harlem Renaissance (which profiled intellectuals and
creatives such as Zora Neale Hurston, Langston Hughes, and
Claude McKay), it was also the center for Marcus Garvey's back
to African movement and a site where the Harlemites rallied for
such international figures like the Ethiopian emperor Haile Selas-
sie. A center of all forms of then experimental music from Jazz
and the Blues, and the home of distinguished American cultural
institutions such as the Cotton Club and Apollo Theatre. Places
where legendary performers such as Duke Ellington, Ella Fitzger-
ald, and many others entertained people from all over the country. Harlem was home to many intellectuals, artists, and activists
who profoundly influenced the cultural and intellectual landscape
of the United States, specifically and more broadly, the African
Diaspora. Harlem was the place of Black consciousness, pride,

and self-determination and occupies a unique place in the imagination of African Americans and the African Diaspora. James Weldon Johnson described Harlem in his prescient essay published in 1925:

> It is true that Harlem is a Negro community, well defined and stable; anchored to its fixed homes, churches, institutions, business, and amusement places; having its own working, business, and professional classes. It is experiencing a constant growth of group consciousness and community feeling. Harlem is, therefore, in many respects, typically Negro (3).

Johnsons' words above were printed twenty-five years after the release of *The Philadelphia Negro: A social study* by W.E.B. Du Bois. The first sociological study of a black neighborhood in the United States, Du Bois began his ethnographic work in 1896 when he was invited to probe the condition of urban black life by the Philadelphia house movement. Du Bois produced one of the most exhaustive empirical studies of black life in America at this point. Recognizing mere structure of the residential patterns of blacks were because of the impact of racism. Du Bois outlined two significant social and political realities espoused by white liberalism that continue to haunt Black America today. He first disavowed the perception that life for black people was better out of the South. He contends:

> Many are the misapprehensions and misstatements as to the social environment of Negroes in a great Northern city. Sometimes, it is said, here they are free; they have the same chance as the Irishman, the Italian, or the Swede; at other times it is said, the environment is such that it is really more oppressive than the situation in southern cities. The student must ignore both of these extreme statements and seek to extract from the complicated mass of facts the tangible evidence of a social atmosphere surrounding Negroes...
>
> (Du Bois 8)

He also acknowledged the higher prices and substandard housing offered to non-whites:

> Ignorance and carelessness...will not explain all or even the greater part of the problem of rent among the Negroes. There

are three causes of even greater importance: these are the limited localities where Negroes rent, the peculiar connection of dwelling and occupation, and the social organization of the Negro. The undeniable fact that most Philadelphia white people prefer not to live near Negroes limits the Negro very seriously in his choice of a cheap home. Moreover, real estate agents, knowing the limited supply, usually raise the rent a dollar or two for Negro tenants if they do not refuse them all together. Again, the occupations which the Negro follows, and which at present he is compelled to follow, are of a sort that makes it necessary for him to live near the best portions of the city: the mass of Negroes are, in the economic world, purveyors to the rich working in private houses, in hotels, large stores, etc. In order to keep this work, they must live nearby... much of the Negro problem in the city finds adequate explanation when we reflect that here is a people receiving a little lower wages than usual for less desirable work and compelled, in order to do that work, to live in a little less pleasant quarters than most people, and pay for them somewhat higher rents.

(Du Bois 295–96)

Du Bois lauded how black-segregated communities were affirming spaces of creative and cultural possibility. However, he forthrightly critiques the white liberals who promoted and encouraged forced segregation. Langton Hughes described the Harlem Renaissance as "the period when the Negro was in vogue." Hughes references the monied white people who flooded that neighborhood to participate in the intellectual salons, jazz clubs, and theaters. At a time when blacks were relegated to specific jobs, with unequal pay and able to find housing only in the designated neighborhood, the white community would travel to black communities "to watch the negros play" and (objectify them). In his ethnography, Du Bois confirmed, what we now call redlining, the discriminatory lending practices that reject mortgages and loans based on race and ethnicity. It is forced segregation that only made housing available in designated segments of the city for black and brown people—and making rents and substandard housing so expensive that it is unattainable and sometimes impossible own a home. Du Bois's ethnography is prescient in that he lays bare a concept that would continue to plague black and brown communities globally, which is the role of capitalism in the forced segregation of black people. Another point of interrogation in Du Bois's scholarship is what he called "the negro problem." He unravels the question, "how does it feel to be a problem?" He questions how laws and law enforcement work to separate the races and traces social policies to archaic colonial histories that forced the enslavement of people of African descent and the annihilation of native communities. The contemporary term of which Du Bois describe, is what we have come to label as structural racism. Du Bois's question, "how does it feel to be a problem," challenges the perception of blackness from the eyes of whiteness. He suggests whiteness considers blackness as a burden, non-contributor to the culture, uncivilized. But the question pivoted to the perspective of blackness, is a negotiation of self-worth in a world that does not acknowledge or value their existence. The Duboisian concept of double consciousness "this sense of always looking at oneself through the eyes of others, of one's soul by the tape of a world that looks on in amused contempt and pity" (Du Bois 45). Often referred to as double vision, it is the internalization of disparaging and derogatory representations of blackness that is circulated globally. "Unable to perceive themselves through their own eyes [they are] unable to measure their own value" (Gordon and Gordon 216). To name Harlem as a mecca for the African Diaspora is complicated. As presented by Du Bois, segregated urbanism does produce an orgy of intellectual feasts, an abundance of creative production, and be a hotbed of political activism and education. But is its forced segregation that is situated in substandard and little maintained housing which offers limited economic development and advancement. What the monied white folks who sojourn to such communities to absorb "culture" of the happy negro witness is, in the terms of de Certeau, tactical performances of the art of making do. Tactics are creative and ingenious ways of marginal communities use to combat and resist the "strategies" of the powerful, such as the landlord, city institutions, government, etc. (Certeau). It is the very act of which Smith articulates at the beginning of this chapter of her life growing up in Belize.

Harlem is sacred for many people of African descent. From the creative production, scholarship, and music, what has come from Harlem has had a profound influence on American culture generally. Du Bois outlined in 1896 that forced segregation and the continued legacy of the degradation of blackness that serves as the bases of law enforcement work in tandem with capitalism in American society to continue the oppression of black people. Du Bois's study would become even more pertinent with the economic and social shifts of the sixties and seventies and still today.

Rhetoric of Redevelopment/Gentrification

Like many major cities in the United States, what began in the late fifties, the large-scale urban decline and neglect were made visible. Communities like Harlem were affected because of their already marginal positionality. The 1980s brought about an increased rhetoric of "fixing a problem," aka redevelopment. In the city of New York, because of the disinvestment in communities due to the loss of population and the city's aggressive tax policy (tax delinquency among landlords), the city ended up owning 60% of the entire housing inventory in Harlem (Van Ryzin and Genn). That coupled with the unhoused challenges, when at a certain point in the eighties the abandoned and empty hotels and boarded up apartments became shelters for the homeless. The national policy toward housing in the United States began to shift from the Roosevelt era's approach that brought about the construction of housing projects as a solution to contain poverty and marginal communities that could not afford housing because of redlining and other discriminatory practices. Using the term "slum clearance," blocks with historical and unique architecture were demolished, and people were displaced to make way for government-owned, large-scale, streamlined, drab, and monolithic buildings. The term "Urban renewal" became synonymous with "negro removal" according to Brent, thus situating blacks and other communities of color as a "problem" (Van Ryzin and Genn). The large-scale public housing and the people who inhabited them became a symbol of the problem. Performance theorist Conquergood wonderfully articulates how the rhetoric of development is used to mark neighborhoods and specific populations to legitimate the removal of people in his ethnography of the Big Red tenement apartment in Chicago in the eighties. Like Big Red, Harlem

> ...Displayed middle-class fears and ambivalences about difference, density, deterioration, and demographic change...Defined as dirty, disorderly, deteriorating, and dangerous, [Harlem] became ripe for redevelopment...Anxiety about dirt and disorder sets the state for the elimination of difference and mobilizes efforts to purge boundaries and purge the environment.
>
> (Conquergood 133–34)

The words such as "dirt, dangerous, and deterioration" spark fear in middle-class (aka white) communities who desired "clean" neighborhoods. The rhetoric suggests a moral obligation to improve the conditions of the city and thus legitimizes the forced removal of people and wholesale destruction of buildings. According to Freeman, from 1950 to 1980, the poverty rate reached nearly 40%, and Harlem lost a third of its population, coupled with disinvestment, Harlem was labeled as a problem neighborhood (26).

The election of Ed Koch brought about an approach rooted in neo-liberalism that would forever change the concept of development, particularly in New York City but specifically for Harlem. The progressive leaning mayor initiated the "ten-year housing program in 1986." Despite the economic downturn of the eighties, the population in New York City was growing; the then mayor sought to increase affordable housing and mitigate growing inequities. Koch subsidized specific components of city government, including housing development. The mayor partnered with the business sector, privatized some public spaces, and deregulated policy to entice developers to work with the city to redevelop the large, abandoned housing stock.

The plan converted low-end rentals to condos and co-ops and aimed at providing affordable housing to a percentage of low-income and midrange-income households. According to the Furman Center report, of all the neighborhoods of New York City, Harlem was the largest transform or redeveloped with 21, 632 unites from 1983 to 2003 ("Housing Policy in New York City: A Brief History"). Some critics suggest the program renovated and refurbished boarded and abandoned properties did nothing more than pave the way for gentrification. The incentivized deregulations which promoted private investment and development and the increased initiatives and subsidies targeted at the middle or market-rate housing and ownership make it unaffordable to lower and midrange middle-class families. The population of Harlem has grown in the last two decades more than any other. However, the population of blacks has decreased (Roberts).

The report from Furman Center also reveals the demographic shift in Harlem. According to the 2020 census, between 2015 and 2019 the neighborhoods black population declined by over 10,000 people (from 62% to 54.3%). In the same time frame, the white population increased from 11.8% to more than 15.5% ("Central Harlem Mn10"). Smith and other activists suggest that gentrification does not have to remove people from the communities but rather redevelop and construct housing that is affordable to those who already reside in the community. The *Dear Dark Skinned Girl*, a blog curated by four young black women from Harlem voice their concerns:

> Gentrification is ultimately problematic because there is a lack of community investment that follows the migrations of these businesses and residents. The resources and money put into integrating these businesses into the Harlem community are not applied to pre-existing infrastructures such as Harlem's several public schools and Black businesses. Although research points to gentrification providing new jobs for urban areas, in several cases these new opportunities are not enough to sustain the original, typically low-income residents of these neighborhoods. Demanding that newly built housing is affordable and relative to the income of the neighborhood's current residents is a solution several community leaders in Harlem and other urban areas are presenting.
>
> (Grant)

The young Harlemites point to the economic, labor and the perseveration of culture that are under threat as the community changes as it is according to Sam Roberts, who penned the *New York Times* article "No Longer Majority Black, Harlem is in Transition". It has changed and is changing but the question posed by artists like Dianne Smith is the identity of Harlem and its sacred place in the African Diaspora. Must gentrification and redevelopment be synonymous with the removal of culture and history of a place? But more importantly for Smith and others is the labeling of people associated with the place and how to work toward the perseveration of culture associated with self-worth. The rhetoric of redevelopment occurs in places labeled as dirty, deteriorating, and detritus, the people who inhabited such places should not be labeled as such. Smith's concept of the "newly assigned value" of objects to preserve the culture of Harlem also creates affirming visual representations of blackness against the rhetoric deployed in favor of gentrification (Figure 7.1).

Smith recalls a conversation with her friend John, who is from the South and has lived in Harlem since 1990. He has furnished his apartment with items mostly savaged from the streets of New York. John says,

> Sixty percent of his treasures were found in Harlem and forty percent downtown. People in both places may have been throwing out things to purge or upgrade nevertheless, he finds better

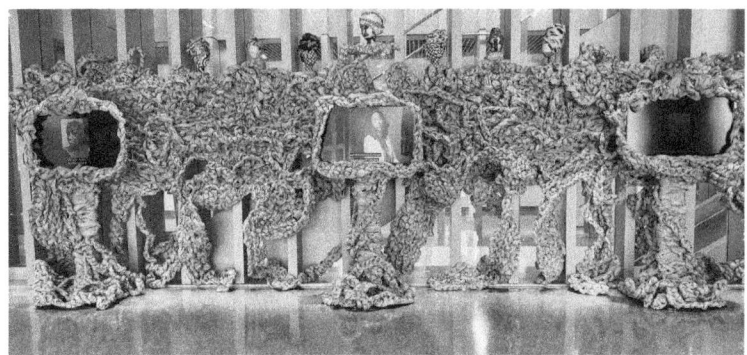

Figure 7.1 Image Credits: Dianne Smith. Installation view. Dianne Smith, STUFF, 2014–2020. Butcher paper, African fabric, Wooden Mannequin Heads, Video. Dimensions Variable. Video Lengths Variable. Imitation of Life, 2015, Video Projection Under the Viaduct JuJu II, 2017, Wood Stump, Embroidery, Nails, Exhibition "Twisted, Woven, Tied", Material For The Arts AIR.

stuff uptown than he does downtown. One reason he believes is that "People downtown know what they are throwing away and don't necessarily care while, people in Harlem do not. They are unaware that they're throwing away expensive antiques like the lamps, chairs and the Serapi rug valued at twenty-five hundred dollars." John admits that the things he finds in the neighborhood he would never "just sit out." His finds are definitely things he would "give to someone else or resell" as he so often does.[4]

Smith's recalling of the interview with John highlights the essence and aim of her work: The preservation of the distinctive Harlem black culture and the affirmation and celebration of black bodies both of which are under assault and in Harlem, on the brink of extinction. Smith's understanding of gentrification is real because through her time living in Central Harlem, she has witnessed the destruction of culturally historic spaces to make way for large-scale commercial buildings and thus moving some of her friends out of the neighborhood. Her work attends to a black neighborhood and a people that has been defined as a problem. Thinking through Du Bois's double consciousness, Smith suggest a "newly assigned value" concept which she explains as, "thinking about objects other than what it was in intended for," but rather to think about the thing beyond it being for what I'm using it for, and how it gets placed."[5] The "value" is complicated and complex as surmised in the conversation with John above, who opines that the Harlemites may not understand the value of objects perhaps because, it reflects how they value themselves visually. Dianne Smith is a cultural archivist who understands the power of "things." Her work not only documents a history that reflects an increasingly shifting community but affirms and values black and brown people and bodies. "One of the things as black people in America and in the world," Smith claims, "is this idea of being seen, or not seen." People must see themselves visual represented and their stories told to bring value to themselves, community, their objects. This segment of the chapter, through teasing through Smith's concept of "newly assigned value" in which she attends to history, social issues, and corporeality, I highlight and discuss the "For Colored Girls" and between "Between Harlem and Me" and "Uptown Parade" installations. Since 2012, butcher paper has figured prominently in her work. Here, I focus on her use of butcher paper and archival images (those often discarded and/or rarely used) to reveal the complicated and nuanced stories of Harlem that attend to social issues and work toward celebrating and affirming blackness. Intellectually, she makes the connections between race and identity particularly corporeality, specifically the essences of skin. The idea emerged when she walked through Wall Street pondering a commissioned work for a show on Governor's Island about the history of African Americans in New York. It was a crake in the sidewalk that propelled the idea of butcher paper.

> I was down on Wall Street area walking and I looked down and I noticed the cracks in the sidewalk. And it occurred to me that crack had a memory, and it had a story. What material could I use to manipulate, and cause that same kind effect? Now one might argue concrete and butcher paper are two different things, but I was really interested in what I considered mark making. And, when I thought about the butcher paper, also, it made sense, … I thought about the African burial ground. And I was like, "Well, I can't talk about the history of African Americans in New York, without talking about the enslaved Africans, and the ports that were in New York." And the fact that crack was on top of a burial ground. And so butcher paper is used to wrap meat. It's about cargo and shipping. It's about commodity. It's fragile, but it's durable. It's easily manipulated.

It can be boxed and pushed into corners. And it made me think of the bodies of enslaved Africans and how some of those same things in ways I described the butcher paper were true, for the enslaved African, and this idea of skin.[6]

The use of the butcher paper, a mundane and utilitarian object that evokes thoughts of black bodies, Smith manipulates and marks the folds and cresses to signify and register a particular narrative about labor, history, and everyday life. She continues:

When you think about your ancestors, your grandmother, your aunties, your mother, extended family, and as their aging and their skin begins to wrinkle, in those wrinkles, their stories, their memories. Some we know, some we'll never know, some that are just a part of us, and we don't even understand how we are moving with those ancestral memories buried in us. And the butcher paper was a way for me to talk about that from a very human perspective.[7]

In 2014, Dianne Smith was commissioned to create a project that would contribute to an exhibition to commemorate the 40th anniversary of Ntozake Shange's, *for colored girls who have considered suicide/when the rainbow is enuf.* Shange, a poet and choreographer, shares the narratives of seven black women. Aptly, described as a choreopoem, *for colored girls* is a series of twenty autoethnography poems performed through movement and recitation by women identified by a color. The topics addressed range from rape and post-traumatic stress disorder to domestic violence. In 1974, it premiered on Broadway, making it the second play was written by a black woman to make it to the leading New York stage. Smith's installation titled "STUFF" is a response to the poem by the lady in green, "somebody almost walked off wid alla my stuff." The poem tackles the issue of domestic violence.

The installation is a wall of densely braided, knotted, and twisted butcher paper with three video monitors. The three documentary-style videos are of different women telling stories. One features a series detailing how "someone walked off with their stuff"—it is a slide show of images documenting the "stuff" in Smiths' apartment and studio. The voice of Smith interpreting Shange accompanies the rapid borage of photographs. The most personal and intimate video is titled "It Happened to Me." Images of Smith's face appear

over and over again. Each provides a unique perspective of her dis-
figured and bruised face. She had made the pictures the evening
of an assault. She claims that she had become comfortable with
documenting things, and it was necessary to document what had
occurred through her own eyes. As the images role, the voice of
Smith is heard reciting statistics of domestic violence, with the
sound of a fist pounding in the background. The assault she references in the video is an incident that occurred the day before the
initial planning meeting for the exhibition. Her 6′6, 270 lb. then boyfriend began to punch her in the face. After he refuses her request
to pack his things and leave her apartment, she is confronted with
calling the police. However, for her, that would risk a big black man
being killed, so she garnered the support of her best friend, who
then called the boyfriend's best friend, who convinced him to pack
his things and leave. She reveals to *Essence Magazine* what happens
the following day as she walks through the neighborhood:

> As she walked down the street of her neighborhood, she noticed
> that something in her had changed. "I had my hat pulled down,
> and I had to ask myself, who am I protecting? Am I worried
> about what people think? But I'd done nothing wrong. There
> was no reason for me to be ashamed." In that moment, Dianne
> decided that if anyone asked her what happened she'd tell them
> the truth.
>
> (Sy Savane)

For Smith, the installation asked all of us to interrogate stuff,
"There's the stuff that is tangible, but then there's the stuff that's
rooted in your spirit, your mental health, your physical health, your
emotional health, and it's ethereal for some."[8] The stuff of what she
speaks is also, not allowing others to take away one's self-worth. The
installation and the narrative surrounding the process of creating
the piece opens the space of dialogue about difficult issues. Smith
herself invites other to engage with the narrative through hearing
and witnessing the narratives on the videos and also the magnitude of the wrapped and knotted butchers paper is an added performance to the presentation. The exhibition has traveled to seven
locations including The Schomburg Center for Research in Black
Culture in Harlem (the first show), Barnard College, and five other
sites in the United States. In each location, the use of butcher paper
takes on the contours of the space and thus takes on a different

meaning. The installation itself reveals a narrative but also the act of creating, making the knots and twists is equally a performance. Smith manipulated more than 6,300 sq feet of paper and took more than thirty hours for the Barnard College install. The movement of her body, the use of her hands, and arms, draw from an archive of her body. She insists,

> Hair braiding, and for me, the motion of my hands creating that work is reminiscent of Granny kneading Johnny Cake or Creole Bread in the mornings or being in the backyard washing very early on the scrub board...The memory of her wringing out the sheets and the clothing, and hanging it on the back line, was special and important to me that I could somehow carry on the traditions of the women in my family, through my hands in that way. Granny's work, not realizing it as a child, was very laborious. She worked hard, but she made it look easy and effortless, and she never complained. So, the work that I do with those installations have a level of labor that is in homage to that labor that she did, every single day.[9]

Smith's performance of making and marking the paper is honoring the often-invisible labor of the women in her community but black women generally. The installation with the butcher paper is an invitation to explore, not only the social issues addressed in *for colored girls* but the political issue of affirming black skin. As articulated earlier, Smith is concerned with black people being seen. Positive visual representation of blackness is a political act in a country that deploys negative and disparaging images as a means of devaluing one's personhood. Just as she does with butcher paper, Smith uses photography to both preserve culture and to create affirming representations of blackness.

Parading Blackness

While compiling research at The Schomburg, Smith was fascinated with the trove of historic images of Harlem. Most of the images in the boxes had not been seen our touched in years, as they were tucked away in the specialized boxes in the temperature control rooms of the research facility. Interesting that such institutions preserve artifacts but rarely present them in publicly assessable ways. I describe as discarded in the sense they are rarely seen and, in some cases, hidden. Similar to what one does with trash. Smith's fascination with the camera is as means of documenting her everyday life.

> Making images is about my relationship to Harlem, and the way I see Harlem, and I see the beauty in the everyday ordinary spaces of Harlem. And for years, I had just been going around snapping a photo here, snapping a photo there, of the things that catch my eye.[10]

Her noninvasive images reflect the happenings on the street corner or the gestural movement of a person as they walk about Lenox avenue. But the access to the archival and historic images encouraged a rethinking or, in her words, newly assigned value of the pictures. Smith's photographic series "Between Harlem and Me" and the public art project "Uptown Parade" are installations that ask the onlooker to examine the landscape of Harlem critically. I will discuss the two projects together because the emphasis is placed on the making and displaying of the images. Smith claims that she is making a home through the images, a space between nostalgia and the contemporary to evoke memories that would give pride of place to create a sense of home for black Harlem. But also, in this particular body of work, she is thinking about what the everyday movement of being black in America is.

> When you think about how ... unfortunately, this is the place in the world that we live in, and that's reality, how we're having to navigate place in space.
> And we exist in the media from either we're doing crimes on the news, and then we are the exceptional black that's the athlete, the entertainer...But the people who are just living in the middle, are the ones that are getting the police called on them for doing regular everyday things like walking down the street, bird watching, walking through a neighborhood eating Skittles, being killed, just regular things....It was important for me to show this idea of normalcy, and the beauty in what is regular and simple for us.[11]

Collage is not the appropriate word for the images Smith creates. She digitally maneuvers the archival and historical images and juxtaposes them with her images. Remarkably, the images site the very same location from 1940 as one from 2017 (Figure 7.2).

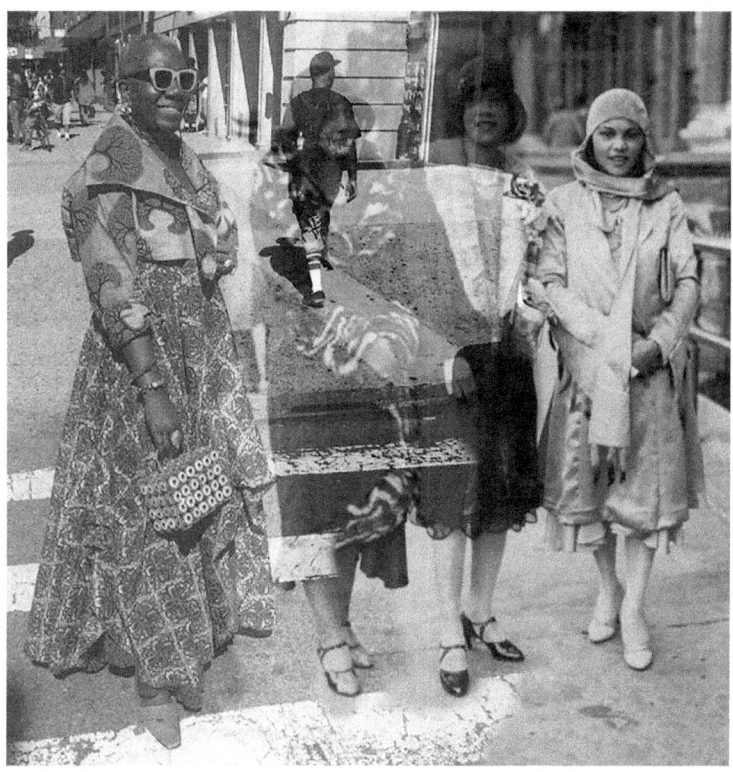

Figure 7.2 Dianne Smith, 2021, Harlem Ladies, 2021, Archival Digital
Pigment Print, 20 × 20. Image Credits: Dianne Smith Schomburg
Archival Images. *Between Harlem and Me Are a Series of Images
from my Most Recent Body of Work. The Montage Overlays my
Photos with Images from The Schomburg's Archives. I Have Been
Documenting Changes and the Impact of Gentrification in my
Harlem Community Since the 1990s. I Need to Normalize Black
and Brown life in America Absent the White Gaze. I Document my
Community as I See it and Connect Between its Past and Present
While Fostering a Conversation with its Future.*

The almost ghostly mirage-like photographs reveal stories of
existence; they document the legacy and history of black people
in rapidly turning white spaces. However, to study the photos,
what a sense of pride in the details of dress, commerce, and play.
In the image titled "Harlem Ladies," a statuesque black woman
adorn a trendy A-framed dress made of green- and gold-toned

Dutch wax African fabrics, with pointed yellow mule shoes and wearing shades that foreground the closely shorn fade hairstyle revealing the emerging streaks of gray hair. It meshes with a black and white image of a group of Black women from the 1930s standing at the identical corner wearing fur-lined coats and scarfs to cover the below-the-knee skirts that expose the Mary Jane low-heel shoes. A fading image of a young black man walking along with his backpack. The image presents the style and beauty of every day—women one could surmise walking about the day, shopping down Lenox avenue, posing, chatting, being seen. In the image, Smith plays with chronography, a looking back in order to move forward. A sentiment that history is not dead and the past is not always past, but very present.

It is a looking back to see an affirming reflection of blackness. Smith uses the same process and technique on a larger scale with the "Uptown Parade" installation. In 2020, at the beginning of the COVID-19 pandemic, responding to how the crisis disproportionately impacted black-owned businesses, Urban Umbrella and Uber Eats enlisted artists, restaurants, and retailers to participate in the creation of an outdoor winterized area of The Renaissance Pavilion in Harlem. Smith commissioned public art project was displayed on the awning of Ruby Vintage, a restaurant on the corner of 137th Street and Adam Clayton Powell Boulevard. Harlem has one of the country's most prominent African American Day parades. The event would normally occur in September to mark the end of summer. Because of the pandemic, the festival was canceled. The parade extends up seventh avenue, right in front of the restaurant and Smith's first Harlem apartment. She decided to bring the parade back to Harlem. Using the same montage technique as with "Between Me and Harlem," Smith made six 96 × 36 panels each that would wrap around the front of the corner restaurant. The installation large in scale transformed that block of the neighborhood. It became a site where parades of people would come to have selfies made. Many were excited to see themselves reflected on the huge awning. Smith's objective is clear: "I am looking at the beauty and the joy of who we are, and the resiliency and the essence of who we are. To be able to show these beautiful black faces in Harlem on a huge platform." And that she does, the meaning of visibility cannot be overlooked particularly in the contemporary moment in Harlem. Smith's use of images about the past with the present on buildings mark and define the urban landscape, thus is a strategy to fight against erasure.

Resisting Death

Culture is rambunctious, infectious, and a contested domain. The vibrant energy of Harlem is the result of the resiliency, labor, creativity, and intellectual fervor of black and brown people who were relegated to that swath of Manhattan. Like Du Bois, Fanon, and other intellectuals before her, Smith comprehends the complexities and complications of cultural politics surrounding place, race, and identity.

When asked about her thoughts of Harlem not being majority black and the wave of white artist taking over spaces, she quips: "I don't think about them. They are so insignificant to how I move through my community, I don't think about them ... I don't think about the others in that way that move here, because for me, Harlem is still quintessentially the Black Mecca."[12] Smith's concept of newly assigned value is a position of recognizing power. For one to be able to look beyond objects, waste, and trash, to have the capacity to consider reuse and multiple meanings of things, one must first understand that they have agency and power to repurpose and rethink "things" in their lives.

As a cultural worker, Smith is asking black people to look at themselves and to look at themselves fully against the backdrop of gentrification and the rhetoric of redevelopments that paints Harlem as dirty, disorganized, and needing to be cleaned. The large-scale images of "Between Harlem and Me" and "Uptown Parade" that document the everyday life of everyday Black Harlemites are a strategic deployment of self-pride, to negotiate double consciousness, and to respond to Du Bois's question of being the problem. And even more so, the use of butcher paper, a textual, physical, and symbolic narrative of black skin. Dianne Smith works toward the empowerment and preservation of the black history and culture of Harlem through rethinking waste and trash.

Note

1 Interview with Dianne Smith, August 21, 2022.
2 Interview with Dianne Smith, August 21, 2022.

3 Interview with Dianne Smith, August 21, 2022.
4 Interview with Dianne Smith, August 21, 2022.
5 Interview with Dianne Smith, August 21, 2022.
6 Interview with Dianne Smith, August 21, 2022.
7 Interview with Dianne Smith, August 21, 2022.
8 Interview with Dianne Smith, August 21, 2022.
9 Interview with Dianne Smith, August 21, 2022.
10 Interview with Dianne Smith, August 21, 2022.
11 Interview with Dianne Smith, August 21, 2022.
12 Interview with Dianne Smith, August 21, 2022.

Works Cited

"Central Harlem Mn10." *Neighborhood Profiles*. NYU Furman Center https://furmancenter.org/neighborhoods/view/central-harlem. Accessed August 23 2022.

Certeau, Michel de. *The Practice of Everyday Life*. University of California Press, 1984. vol. Book, Whole.

Conquergood, Lorne Dwight and E. Patrick Johnson. *Cultural Struggles: Performance, Ethnography, Praxis*. University of Michigan Press, 2013. E. Patrick Johnson and E. P. Johnson, vol. Book, Whole.

Du Bois, W. E. B. *The Philadelphia Negro*. vol. no. 14, Kraus-Thomson Organization Ltd, 1973. vol. Book, Whole.

———. and Donald B. Gibson. *The Souls of Black Folk*. Penguin Books, 1996. vol. Book, Whole.

Freeman, Lance. *There Goes the 'Hood: Views of Gentrification from the Ground Up*. Temple University Press, 2006. vol. Book, Whole.

Gordon, Lewis R. and Jane Anna Gordon. *Not Only the Master's Tools: African-American Studies in Theory and Practice*. Paradigm, 2006. vol. Book, Whole.

Grant, Jada. "How Gentrification Is Stripping Harlem of Its Culture." vol. 2022, *Dear Dark Skinned Girl* 2021 https://deardarkskinnedgirl.com/2021/01/24/harlemgentrifcation/.

"Housing Policy in New York City: A Brief History." *Working Paper No.06-01*. Furman Center for Real Estate and Urban Policy https://furmancenter.org/files/publications/AHistoryofHousingPolicycombined0601_000.pdf.

Hughes, Langston. *Collected Works of Langston Hughes, Vol. 13: The Big Sea: An Autobiography*. University of Missouri Press, 2002. vol. Book, Whole.

Roberts, Sam. "No Longer Majority Black, Harlem Is in Transition." *New York Times* https://tinyurl.com/2p8n472p. Accessed August 23 2022.

Smith, Dianne. "Trash, Consumption, Class and the Politics of Race." *Creative Practice*, vol. MFA, Transart Institute, 2012.

Strasser, Susan. *Waste and Want: A Social History of Trash*. First ed., Metropolitan Books, 1999. vol. Book, Whole.

Sy Savane, Erickka. "How Dianne Smith Turned a Domestic Violence Incident into Art." *Essence Magazine* https://www.essence.com/culture/dianne-smith-domestic-violence-art/. Accessed August 23 2022.

Thompson, M. *Rubbish Theory: The Creation and Destruction of Value.* Oxford University Press, 1979. vol. Book, Whole.

Van Ryzin, Gregg G. and Andrew Genn. "Neighborhood Change and the City of New York's Ten-Year Housing Plan." *Housing Policy Debate*, vol. 10, no. 4, 1999, pp. 799–838.

8   The Anti-Museum

There's too much violence, and it's super unpredictable and nobody casually talks about how hard it is to get over it. People just incorporate a lot of violence into the ordinariness of their existence, but it's really stressful and painful.

—Vanessa German, Interview with the author

The anti-museum according to Mbembe is "by no means is it an institution but rather the figure of another place, one of radical hospitality. A place of refuge … a place of unconditional rest and asylum for all the rejects of humanity and the 'wretched of the earth'" (172). I have written about such spaces within the framing of the performance of possibility in the context of Haiti after the devastating earthquake of January 2010. I defined the performance of possibility as events or moments that evoke feelings of hope—a belief in a sheer promise of what could be, even against an undercurrent of proclaimed despair. It is more than just an idyllic sentimentalism but a practical concept of the here and now that informs a visualizing of a promise, a yearning for what can or will come (Beasley "From Haiti: Gounda Gounda, the Ghetto Biennale and the Performance of Possibility.") I wrote those thoughts against the ruin and debris of the already fragmented lives of the Haitian community. Yet, I witnessed possibility in the Haitian community's capacity to be in the present, to enact stories of the event over and over to give voice to the trauma so as not to allow it to settle in the body but to envision a better life beyond the here and now and use the adversity to push forward. What I witnessed in Haiti, and what was more pronounced to me during that time, was the sheer notion of how the body is an archive. It is a repository of everyday interactions that we reference to make sense of our existence. It is also like a museum of old dead experiences that linger and need

DOI: 10.4324/9780429028489-8

to be discarded (Harris et al.). Because of the dispersal, disloca-
tion, and colonialism of people of African descent are hindered in
professing the fullness of their pain, according to Mbembe, "for
an incomplete, partial and fragmented archive" built on faulty
premises (160). It is a fragmented and inaccurate archive because it
was assembled in part by someone else which limits possibility. In
the remaining pages, I wish to dwell on the concept of the performance of possibility and the strategy of care as a tactic of survival.
Through their sculptures, Vanessa German and Simone Leigh tell
stories of possibility. Thus, they built spaces to enable BIPOC to
speak for and affirm themselves through the acknowledgment of
their bodies. They build on the fragmented archive to produce are-
nas of care and anti-museums.

Corporeal Narrative

Narratives are powerful. They define identities, places, and for
some, the realities in which they live. Stuart Hall and Michel-Rolph
Trouillot, sons of the Caribbean, spoke to the constricting power of
the narrative and how black subjects efficiently perform the ascribed
debased script of colonialism; they theorized ways of constructing
different and affirming narratives from the debris and traces of the
remains. To perform the archive is to consider that bundle of dis-
cursivity that surrounds and flows through the body. The discursiv-
ity of which Foucault speaks is the panoply of rhetorical discourses
in the form of tropes and stereotypes cast on marginal communities. The discourse is so profound and repeated that it becomes
internalized. The body archives one's history, pain, and pleasures.
It is performed through the utterances of the body—the gait, gesture, voice, language, accents, etc. To speak of possibility and claim
a positionality of care is to equip oneself with the tools necessary
to construct new narratives and internal monologues. Mbembe's
ultimate critique of Western humanism is found in its premise that
all knowledge begins with the white European historical record,
and all others simply do not exist or are subjected to debasement.
Fanon was preoccupied with the effects of foregrounding and the
entrenched (and thus performance) of the colonial narrative on people of African descent. According to Mbembe, Western humanism
is not a historical record at all but rather, a "book of atrocities. It is
also the mourning of what was lost, in a way that does not dwell in
the trauma, in a way that allows the survivor to escape the cures of
repetition" (161). Slavery, colonialism, and capitalism are systems

that ascribe a "social death." A death that convinces individuals into believing that their lives are without value and work to strip black bodies of value and to consider them waste and discarded matter (Mbembe). A guiding question of Fanon, Mbembe too, is how to prevent this cycle of black bodies believing in the narrative of debasement. The performance of possibility is a catholicon and a strategy to combat the persistence of a social death. German and Leigh use their creative facility to construct spaces of healing and thereby construct narratives of hope.

Healing Room/Art House

Simone Leigh is the first black woman to represent the United States at the Venice Biennale, where she was awarded the silver dove, the highest honor bestowed at the international art fair. A ceramicist by training, her sculptural installations play with historical materials to bridge a nuanced understanding of the past with the present (Figure 8.1). At the 2014 Dak'art Biennale, Leigh's installation displayed cowrie shells in various hues. An object once considered currency in Africa—now regarded as worthless, the precious and delicate seashells in her work challenges schematic reading for a psych-sexual and diasporic reading (body parts such as an eye,

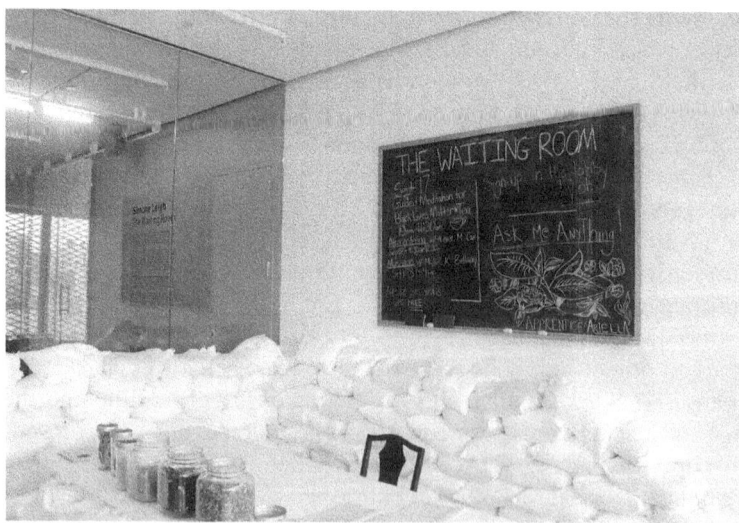

Figure 8.1 From Simone Leigh's *The Waiting Room*. Photograph by Dianne Smith.

anus, a vagina, a mouth) of the object. Leigh's work builds on past sentiments to suggest that the past is always present. Black female subjectivity and its interplay with the archive and history is usually both a theme and method of her portfolio. At the 2022 Venice Biennale, Leigh transformed the US Pavilion designed into a Monticello-styled house—read plantation mansion constructed by enslaved people—using raffia, changing the structure to resemble a 1930s West African dwelling. Her work is often considered "socially engaged" and referred to as a "public servant" because her work attends to contemporary social issues. But according to Leigh,

> I don't feel like a public servant—I would never describe myself as anyone's servant because I'm a black woman and part of the history of free forced labor that this country is built on. However, I do feel that I have a particular responsibility to my community because of who I am and where I live.

(Burton 2016)

Leigh interrogates the past to advance a critical awareness of the present.

An example of Leigh's creative capacity to create spaces of care was her response to the *New York Times* article about Esmin Green, a black woman who collapsed after waiting twenty-four hours in the emergency room (Buckley; Elizabeth A. Harris; Hartocollis). Hospital footage revealed that her body lay on the floor for more than an hour before it was removed. Waiting to be cared for may have killed her. So moved by this story, in 2014, Leigh converted the home of the first African American woman OB-GYN, Josephine English, into a "Free people's medical clinic" in Brooklyn ("Medicine: Simone Leigh in Collaboration with Stuyvesant Mansion"). The space provided free services such as pap smears, HIV testing, free yoga, and dance classes. But in 2016, a similar project on a larger scale was realized at the New Museum aptly titled "Simone Leigh: The Waiting Room." Labeled as an exhibition, the focus of the Waiting Room was "on the rights and roles of women of color in expanding the notions of medicine within a socio-political state of deferred health justice" ("Simone Leigh: The Waiting Room"). The museum was transformed into a space for women's health for six weeks. In addition to free test opportunities, there was a calendar for yoga and dance classes, an herbalist apothecary, movement studios, and public and private healing sessions. Leigh labors to change the narrative by creating spaces of possibility by urging black people, women, in particular, to acknowledge the worth and value of their bodies. She claims that "creating a space for wellness may require both the making of a sanctuary and an act of disobedience against the systematic enactment and repudiation of black pain."[1] Whereas Leigh powerfully transforms traditional cultural centers, German creates spaces of possibility in her local neighborhood (Figure 8.2).

Vanessa German is a multidisciplinary artist in the true sense of the word. From spoken word poetry, vocal performance, and acting to the visual arts, from collage to what she is most known for, the power figure sculptures made from mostly found objects. German is a compelling storyteller. When German moved into the Homewood neighborhood of Pittsburgh (the community of legendary artists such as Billy Strayhorn, Ahmad Jamal, and the setting of John Edgar Wideman novels) and when the basement ceilings became too low for her sculptures, she began constructing the powerful figures on the porch of her home. People, mostly the children in the neighborhood, would stop and watch her work. After a while, a mass of children would come by, watch her work, and ask her

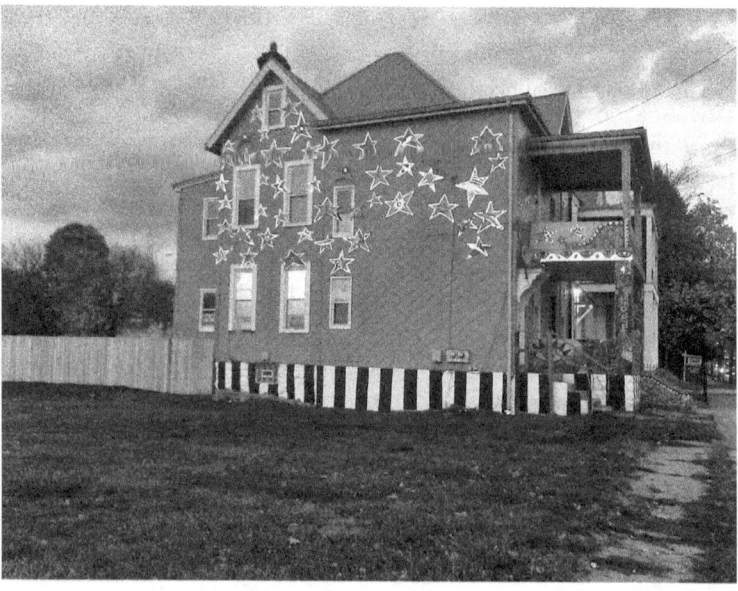

Figure 8.2 Vanessa German's "Art House." Photograph by Vanessa German.

questions. Soon German gave them art supplies and asked them to be creative with her. Eventually, German purchased the neighboring 1905 Victorian house at the corner of the block and rehabbed it into a community space, the Art House (Figure 8.2).

Like her aesthetically nuanced and palimpsestic power figures emit the energy of love, affirmation, and truth, German's Instagram feed is a testament to her conviction that art can heal and reframe the internal dialogue of black lives. At the height of the COVID-19 shutdown in the United States, on most Sunday mornings, German would invite the public into her lush garden; as she waters and prunes, she would sometimes break out in song, poetry, and an extended commentary on local or national events. The narratives are so intimate, sometimes about the little watermelon she attempts to save or the phone call from Miss—a neighbor calling to inform German of a pound cake that she has prepared for her. And sometimes, she addresses violence. Like the death of Mr. Jeff, a person in the community that everyone knew, who was shot in the middle of the street facing the side of the Art House early one morning. He had been recently released from jail and shared his changed life with many. According to German, "the older people knew him from when he was in high school. They may have known his mom. He was somebody's brother. He was somebody's son."[2] This incident occurred after German spent weeks making "Stop the shooting, we love you" signs and posted them throughout the community. "I thought just believing in the power of love that maybe somebody, a shooter, would see that sign and would be so surprised they'd think about the person who they loved who would not ever want them to be a murderer."[3] Mr. Jeff was murdered on a Sunday, on Mother's Day.

The children witnessed the dead body lying in the street. Two days after his murder, at the Art House, the children prepared a memorial for Mr. Jeff by placing blue balloons on the stop sign. When one young boy says, "That's exactly where he fell," pointing to the bloodstain that remains on the asphalt, another responds, "you're not supposed to talk about things like that." German intercedes, "by telling him not to talk about it doesn't make it go away," and one asks "what do you do?" To which German replays, "Well, I make things ... but it also helps to talk to somebody." As the children returned to painting and drawing, they told stories about "being scared of shootings or when somebody died."[4]

The sky-blue painted house is punctuated with glittering stars with the mosaic trim, which is a preview of the interior of the house

with the word "HOPE" outlined on the pillars. The Art House occupies the first floor. The eliminations of walls configured the L-shaped
floor plan. One portion is considered the reading room; the rest is an
open space for creativity. There are no "official hours" at the house
but usually open a couple of days of the week or more depending on
the children and, of course, the schedule of German. It is not a non-
profit but is financed by German herself. In addition to the open Art
House hour, German established a residency program for BIPOC
and LGBTQIA+ artists. She often hosts play readings, a weekly
monologue group, and even stage readings in the backyard where
German provides stage equipment, video projection, bleachers, and
a huge tent. "So it's really casual, and its casual as a set of stairs. You
come in. You sit down and make something ... Nobody is going to
charge you any money. It's almost like having an open studio with
a front door, and anybody who wants to come in comes in," says
German.[5] The Art House is a place for healing and hope.

German and Leigh are cultural workers who carve out spaces
of rest, resistance, and renewal to reimage possibility as a strategy to survive and live. By foregrounding the body, the black body,
they announce the precious and precarious nature of living in an
anti-black world. During the span of writing and research for this
book, two significant events occurred that demonstrate the gravity
and vastness of Mbembe's concept: George Floyd and COVID-19.
The mistreatment and blatant violence deployed against black people is familiar. Still, the circularity of the video depicting Floyd's
death triggered a global rupture—inciting conversations surrounding anti-racism, decolonization, and white supremacy. COVID-19
revealed the ever-expanding gap in accessibility to quality health
care. Even amidst free testing and vaccines, a plethora of barri-
ers (transportation, locality, etc.) exists for the expansive number
of black and brown people who are convinced that nothing is
truly free. On the first anniversary of the death of Floyd, Vanessa
German led a series of blue walks from Pittsburgh to Charlottes-
ville, Virginia, and Omaha, Nebraska; the walks honored Floyd,
Mclain, Taylor, and other hundreds of missing and slain people of
color. In Pittsburgh, the women wore royal blue dresses of various styles. Gathering at the Art House, that group walked and
danced through the neighborhood to the Frick Pittsburgh Museum
(Figure 8.3). As the group walked, they would engage in a call and
response with German, who would shout, "We love one another,
we love this earth. George Floyd, we love you." Often, she would
shout, "Mama, Mama!" and "I can't breathe!" As they processed,

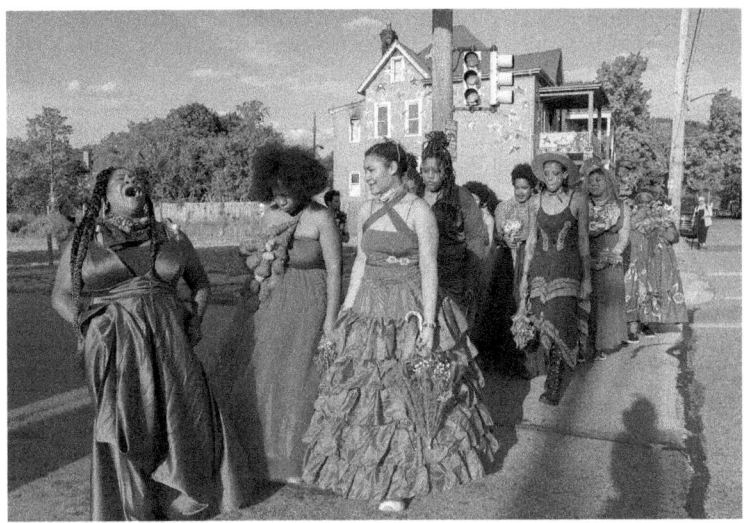

Figure 8.3 Vanessa German Blue Walk at Frick Museum, Pittsburgh, PA, 2021. Heather Mull Photography.

when passing a person of color, they would stop and say, "We love you" (Dague). De Certeau opined that even walking a simple walk-through town could be a revolutionary act (Certeau).

The artists in this book outlined and addressed critical issues and concerns regarding the precarious nature of black lives. The artists foreground the return to the body, a sincere recognition of self that will encourage one to speak their truths and reality, which will precipitate the reframing of the colonial narrative, fill in spaces of the archive, and thus imagine a new possibility. The artists in this text labor to create anti-museums, spaces of radical hospitality, refuge, and rest to combat the anti-black world. A favorite room in German's Art House is the bathroom. "The whole bathroom is mosaic. And around the mirror, there's text, and it's all glass mosaic. And it says, You are so beautiful, yes, you. You are so beautiful …. and around the electrical outlet, it says, "You have power."[6]

Notes

1 Myron Beasley interview with Vanessa German, June 26, 2020.
2 Myron Beasley interview with Vanessa German, June 26, 2020.
3 Myron Beasley interview with Vanessa German, June 26, 2020.

4 Myron Beasley interview with Vanessa German, June 26, 2020.
5 Myron Beasley interview with Vanessa German, June 26, 2020.
6 Myron Beasley interview with Vanessa German, June 26, 2020.

Works Cited

Beasley, Myron M. "From Haiti: Gounda Gounda, the Ghetto Biennale and the Performance of Possibility." *ElSE: The Journal of Art, Literature, and Philosophy*, 2014, vol. 0, pp. 104–11.

Buckley, Cara. "A Life Celebrated, and a City Criticized." *New York Times* https://www.nytimes.com/2008/07/07/nyregion/07funeral.html. 2022.

Burton, Johanna et al. *Public Servants: Art and the Crisis of the Common Good*. The MIT Press, 2016.

Certeau, Michel de. *The Practice of Everyday Life*. University of California Press, 1984. vol. Book, Whole.

Dague, Tyler. "George Floyd among Those Honored in Vanessa German's 'Blue Walk' to the Frick Pittsburgh." *Pittsburgh Post Gazette* https://www.post-gazette.com/ae/art-architecture/2021/05/28/blue-walk-pittsburgh-vanessa-german-the-frick-arthouse-george-floyd-teaira-whitehead/stories/202105270202. Accessed June 12 2022.

Hall, Stuart. *Essential Essays, Volume 2: Identity and Diaspora*. Duke University Press, 2018. Morley David, vol. Book, Whole.

——— and David Morley. *Essential Essays*. Duke University Press, 2019. vol. Book, Whole.

Harris, Elizabeth A. "Ex-Hospital Worker Accused of Cover-up in Patient's Death." *New York Times* https://www.nytimes.com/2011/05/17/nyregion/ex-hospital-worker-accused-of-cover-up-in-patients-death.html.

Harris, V.S. et al. *Refiguring the Archive*. Kluwer Academic Publishers, 2002. vol. Book, Whole.

Hartocollis, Anemona. "Video of Dying Mental Patient Being Ignored Spurs Changes at Brooklyn Hospital." *New York Times* https://www.nytimes.com/2008/07/02/nyregion/02hosp.html.

Mbembe, Achille and Steve Corcoran. *Necropolitics*. Duke University Press, 2019. vol. Book, Whole.

"Medicine: Simone Leigh in Collaboration with Stuyvesant Mansion." https://creativetime.org/projects/black-radical-brooklyn/artists/simone-leigh/#:~:text=with%20Stuyvesant%20Mansion-, Free%20People's%20 Medical%20Clinic, and%20African%20American%20object%2Dmaking. Accessed June 12 2022.

"Simone Leigh: The Waiting Room." *The New Museum* https://www.newmuseum.org/exhibitions/view/simone-leigh-the-waiting-room.

Trouillot, Michel-Rolph and Hazel V. Carby. *Silencing the Past: Power and the Production of History*. Beacon Press, 2015. vol. Book, Whole.

Afterword

Why do the living perform death? Why does every human community have an art of death and dying? What do we, the living—especially those whose lives are saturated with death and dying—learn from such performance? And what, in doing so, do we offer those to come?

Myron Beasley's conception of performance—"the *doing* and the engagement *with*"— has an insight for reflection on its relationship to art and death. That there is the concept of "performance art" suggests a separation of the two, where there is "art" that is not "performance" and performances that are not art, or at least artistic. What, however, if art and performance were not separable, and the human being without either were a performative contradiction? Wouldn't their separation release a form of death—strangely, a death that lurked beneath death even as portrayed in living performance?

Among the many vestiges of Euromodern colonization is the restriction of normative life and, indeed, the very notion of human forms of living. Reduced to conceptions of things onto which properties are placed, the human being, under that model, becomes a blank slate or *tabula rasa* of imagined life that is, in reality, a living death. More, from this model, there is a conception of human completeness as a thing onto which relations or connections—in a word, life—intrude. What is left, then, is the presumed necessary as that which could enable only the material continuation of biological processes. This view treats meaning and value as epiphenomenal or inessential features of human existence.

An immediate response, however, is that human existence without meaning and value or the mythopoetics of life, is no existence at all. Although to exist—from *ex* (forth, out) and *sistere* (to stand)—means to stand out, to appear, it also means to live. But "living" is not an exclusively biological process. Take art, meaning, and value out of human existence, and the human being, although biologically alive, would be suffering a paradoxical living death. Extract those features from human existence long enough, human beings would walk into a pit of despair. Death becomes solace.

The human being, understood from this observation on meaning, is active, dynamic, and relational. Human beings *live* in and through human worlds, and those produce mirrored realities of meaning for us. Yes, there is a narcissistic dimension to this. In every human artifact, in every human action, there is humanity reflecting and living human reality. We could call this condition "good narcissism," since it is how we spend our time from being born human beings into learning how to become human. That is the paradox of our existence. Becoming human means devoting a lot of time paying attention to our teachers who, across the ages, continue to be "us." The expression of human reality is such, then, that to live, we need to do so with or among one another.

Problematic narcissism or narcissistic disorder, however, is the one in which there is a rejection of the sociality of human existence, and the only image in which one places value is one's individual self—understood as complete and godlike. Thus, at the heart of that turning away is a profound misanthropy in which there is narcissistic rage against humanity for the sake of the overly invested self.

Such is what was unleashed in Euromodern colonialism. Frantz Fanon stated it well in his first book, *Black Skin, White Masks* (1952). The concomitant inflation of the ego of Euromodern men and women as "superior" and the attack on all others as "inferior" led to the problem of a world in which there are those who stand "above" humanity and those forced "below." Where then stand human beings? Fanon held no punches. Such a performative effort, he argued, was no less than the attempted murder of humanity.

This attempted murder carried a system of values that are, paradoxically, anti-values. The anti-values attempt to separate symbolic life—affective communication, art, love, meaning, pleasure—from what is presumed ontologically basic. This effort is dehumanization—and the oppression and suffering it fosters through limiting the options of creativity and expressive manifestations of what it means to live a livable human life—have been contested by those upon whom it was imposed throughout.

Beyond the historical impositions, however, is the radical significance of death as not only on the horizon of what is to come, but also that of what preceded all. Among the existential challenges of human existence is, in other words, that reality could get along fine without us. Even more, we *didn't have to come into existence.* Thus, there is a form of pre-death that haunts all birth and subsequent life. This is performed or ritualized in our mythologies and various practices of internment—think, for example, of the expression "from dust to dust." We could add "from pre-anything to no longer anything." There is a "return," even though, at birth, whoever "we" are didn't precede us. Death, then, is a reminder of why we shouldn't take ourselves *too* seriously, for doing so separates us from reality. Pre-death haunts our existence. It, in effect, brings humility to us, and what is humility but, as its etymological roots in dirt or soil attest, our humanity?

The paradoxical haunting of life by pre-death raises the question of "good death," as the Irmandade Nossa Senhora da Boa Morte or Sisterhood of Our Lady of the Good Death phrase it, which makes no sense without understanding that life is our decision to live. We can bring to life what transcends exclusively biological living. This means what we "are" is not a thing or things but, instead, the ongoing, living project of producing meaning and possibility. Art, then, is not an exclusive activity of specialists. It is the human condition, and artists are but those among us who make that reality explicit.

Beasley offered us, then, in this wonderful meditation/performance, a Black existential focus on what is at stake when closure instead of openness is placed upon people marked for "bad death," a death without redemption, a bad faith death of, basically, never having lived because instrumentalized as things for use, as commodities, as there for use from alienated conditions of value. But that attitude, Beasley rightly attests from the outset, is from an *imposed* perspective instead of the lived-reality of those onto whom that imposition is made. From the grandiose to the everyday or the ordinary to the subterranean, psychoanalytical modes and nodes of desire, there is, at each moment, human resistance, resilience, and resuscitation.

The death project of Euromodern colonialism placed at least four interrogatives on Black existence: What does it mean to be human? What does it mean to be liberated and free? Is justification justifiable when it was rallied against Black existence? And is redemption closed? That across Africa, Asia, Oceana, and Indigenous North America and South America death was predominantly marked by the color white brings to the fore the damage done by throwing the cloak of abjection onto blackness. What is blackness, whether in Berlin, Germany, or in Cachoeira of Bahia, Brazil, or in Cape Town, South Africa, or in Dakar, Senegal, or in Harare, Zimbabwe, or in Jacmel, Haiti, or in Port of Spain, Trinidad, or in New York

City in the USA, but where one goes to find life that understands, as Nathalie Etoke wrote in *Melancholia Africana* (2010 in French; 2019 in English), what it means to "for/give"? To give-for and to for-give, whose ambiguity is marked by the slash, reach forth for possibility—with the focus on *giving*—which is nothing short of life living. In such dynamic relationships, vibrant even when otherwise abandoned, there is the production of spaces transformed into places where, through kindness, love, and welcoming among one another as conditions of possibility, humanity belongs and lives.

To give so radically, however, means to give so much that it hurts. To give with such realization is radical love. It is to let go of self-contained, problematic narcissistic representation, of ongoing similitude and sameness, and release possibility for the emergence of freedom to come on its own terms and not yet known forms. It is to acknowledge forces and others greater than oneself and embrace our ability to love difference.

Yet art is also performance of belonging, even when interrogating displacement and disorientation. Despite the vast, uncaring material realities, whether as universe or multiverse, whether as galaxies or massive collapses of energy into indecipherable kinds of stuff, where no one seems to matter, here, on our tiny planet, in the speck of dust we could call "us," there is production by us *for us* offered for value and from which to be valued. What is this performance, analogically, but the reminder, at every moment a Black performs without worry of recognition, of the bankruptcy and fraud of dehumanization? There, in each moment of joy and those of sorrow, from the beautiful to the ugly, from the wonderous to the banal, is the human being reflecting relationships that could only be denied by fellow human beings in bad faith. Each act of signification unveils the lies of dehumanization, and the violent effort to compel submission, to behave as without a right to exist, relies on its own contradictions; the biggest losers, as any analyst of narcissistic disorders would attest, tend to shout the loudly their claim to stand among the gods. To do so against humanity, however, is a loss that is also human, since, as we know, perfecting is our effort, but imperfection and incompleteness our lot.

Paradoxically, artists remind humanity of being a work in progress, of being, in a word, art, or at least artistic. Through his creative engagement with the artists/art in this poignant book, Beasley reminds us of the same. For that, what more to give but proverbial thanks?

Lewis R. Gordon

Index

Note: *Italic* page numbers refer to figures and page numbers followed by "n" denote endnotes.

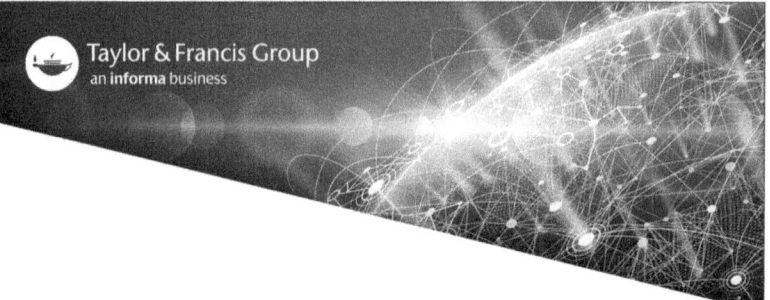
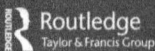
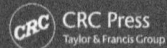

For Product Safety Concerns and Information please contact our EU
representative GPSR@taylorandfrancis.com
Taylor & Francis Verlag GmbH, Kaufingerstraße 24, 80331 München, Germany